THE WORLD IN THE VIKING AGE

Edited by Søren M. Sindbæk & Athena Trakadas

 The Viking Ship Museum in Roskilde 2014

The World in the Viking Age

Edited by Søren M. Sindbæk & Athena Trakadas
© The Viking Ship Museum and the authors 2014
Danish translations: Tríona Nicholl & Athena Trakadas
Design and layout: Carl-H.K. Zakrisson & Tod Alan Sporl
Printed in Denmark by Narayana Press, Gylling
ISBN: 978-87-85180-70-4

Published with support from:
Dronning Margrethes og Prins Henriks Fond
Augustinus Fonden
D/S Orients Fond

Publications by
The Viking Ship Museum
Vindeboder 12
DK-4000 Roskilde, Denmark

Additional photo credits
pp. 12-13: Werner Karrasch © Viking Ship Museum in Roskilde.
pp. 38-39: The David Collection, Copenhagen, Denmark. Inv. no. 27/2003.
pp. 66-67: © Istanbul University Yenikapı Shipwrecks Project Archive.
pp. 92-93: © Trustees of the British Museum.
pp. 9, 19, 24, 44, 63, 70: © Viking Ship Museum in Roskilde.

All dates in the volume are abbreviated
BCE / CE = Before Common Era / Common Era
AH = *Anno Hegirae* (in the year of the *hijra*)

ANTON ENGLERT • LOUISE KÆMPE HENRIKSEN • SØREN M. SINDBÆK • ANNE C. SØRENSEN • ATHENA TRAKADAS

Foreword

Many of the sea routes that connect the world were discovered long before modern history begins. At that time, known in Northern Europe as the Viking Age, unknown oceans across the world were being transformed into familiar waters where sailing ships travelled with ease between nascent towns and harbours. These ships, laden with cargo and with seafarers who met foreign cultures, created unexpected connections between people from the Arctic Circle to the oceans south of the equator.

Some travel accounts have handed down glimpses of these voyages to the present day. However, it is archaeological discoveries in particular which uncover the story of Viking-Age seafaring and voyages of exploration. In recent years, finds from ships, harbours and trading towns around the world have provided new insights into the changes that took place among coastal societies, during a time known in many places as a dark period between antiquity and modern civilisation.

This book was created together with a special exhibition at the Viking Ship Museum in Roskilde. *The World in the Viking Age* reveals a world history concerning ships, people and objects on the move. It is a story that challenges entrenched ideas about the past and present, and about the skills and opportunities of previous generations. The Viking Ship Museum's unique archaeological collection of ships and boats is world renowned as a part of Scandinavian cultural heritage. The fact that this maritime culture and technology is also part of a global story is less well known.

The book and exhibition have been produced with help from researchers from five continents. A close cooperation with the research project *Entrepot* at Aarhus University and the University of York, Great Britain – an initiative financed by the Danish Council for Independent Research's researchers career programme, Sapere Aude – has been particularly helpful in giving the exhibition a strong foundation. This cooperation also included an international research conference, which took place in April 2013, contributing invaluable knowledge to *The World in the Viking Age*.[1] Many of the new results that are presented in the book and exhibition are the culmination of the *Entrepot* project's exploration of maritime exchange networks and urbanisation from the North Atlantic to the Indian Ocean.

This exhibition project would not have been possible without the generous support of the following foundations: Dronning Margrethes og Prins Henriks Fond, Augustinus Fonden, D/S Orients Fond, and Knud Højgaards Fond.

Finally, sincere thanks to Tinna Damgård-Sørensen, director of the Viking Ship Museum, for confidence in the project, and fair wind throughout.

SØREN M. SINDBÆK
Introduction: The World in the Viking Age 8

OHTHERE'S WORLD

JANET BATELY
Ohthere's voyages 14

SØREN M. SINDBÆK
The making of the Viking Age 21

ANTON ENGLERT
Scandinavian ships and seafaring 26

ANTON ENGLERT
Opening up the Northern Seas: the Gokstad ship 30

SARAH CROIX
The loom and the sail 32

DRIES TYS
The Low Countries and the Northern Seas 34

STEVEN P. ASHBY & ASHLEY COUTU
Arctic resources and urban networks 36

ABHARA'S WORLD

DIONISIUS A. AGIUS
Abhara's voyages 40

TIMOTHY POWER
The Abbasid Indian Ocean trade 46

STEPHANIE WYNNE-JONES
Africa's emporia 50

JEREMY GREEN & ATHENA TRAKADAS
Ships of the Indian Ocean 54

TOM VOSMER
The Belitung shipwreck and *Jewel of Muscat* 58

JULIAN WHITEWRIGHT
Maritime rhythms of the monsoon 62

JASON HAWKES & STEPHANIE WYNNE-JONES
India in Africa 64

HELLE HORSNÆS
Changing hands: the Skovsholm dirham hoard 65

Overleaf: *Gaia*, a Norwegian-built reconstruction of the Gokstad ship, an archaeological find dating to the late 9th century (Photo: Svein Olav Løberg, boat guild GAIA).

THEODOSIOS' WORLD

JONATHAN SHEPARD
Theodosios' voyages   68

SAURO GELICHI
The sea of Venice: new cities and the Adriatic Mediterranean economy   74

UFUK KOCABAŞ
Constantinople's Byzantine harbour: the Yenikapı excavations   78

ATHENA TRAKADAS
A sea in transition: ships of the Mediterranean   82

IŞIL ÖZAİT-KOCABAŞ
The Yenikapı 12 wreck: connecting Constantinople   86

JONATHAN SHEPARD & J.-C. CHEYNET
The seals of Theodosios   88

HELLE HORSNÆS
Theophilos' coin: treasure and image   90

NETWORKS

UNN PEDERSEN
Kaupang: Viking-Age expansion to the North   96

MATEUSZ BOGUCKI
Truso, silver and trade   98

CHRIS LOWE
The Inchmarnock 'Hostage Stone'   100

SVEN KALMRING
Hedeby from the sea-side   102

J.C. MOESGAARD & OLE KASTHOLM
Making new money: the Hedeby coin   104

KRISTOFFER DAMGAARD
Aylah, "Palestine's harbour on the China Sea"   106

SORNA KHAKZAD & ATHENA TRAKADAS
The world in a grain of sand: Siraf   108

STEPHANIE WYNNE-JONES, ALISON CROWTHER & MARK HORTON
Zanzibar: a network society   111

JOHN MIKSIC
The Srivijaya Empire and its maritime aspects   115

JUN KIMURA
Seafaring in the Far East   118

SØREN M. SINDBÆK
Suzhou, China, and the Maritime Silk Road   121

SØREN M. SINDBÆK & ATHENA TRAKADAS
The journey of ideas   124

Notes   126

References   130

Index   136

List of authors   137

SØREN M. SINDBÆK

Introduction: The World in the Viking Age

The Viking Age was ignited by the art of building seaworthy sailing ships and the skills to sail them on the open sea. The growth in seafaring, trade, piracy, and exploration that began to gather momentum during the 8th century was not limited to Europe's northern seas, though. It was echoed in other parts of the world at the same time. If the era that began with the great European voyages of discovery at the end of the 15th century is known as the Age of Exploration, then the Viking Age deserves equal claim to the same moniker. From the South China Sea to the North Atlantic, the centuries leading up to the year 1000 were exploration's first great age – a time when ships found routes to uncharted waters, new lands were discovered, and new ports sprang up along coasts.

Seafarers Three accounts of seafarers, who sailed at roughly the same time during the middle of the 9th century, demonstrate how ships both connected and changed the world during the Viking Age. The first of the three, the Norwegian Ohthere, appeared as a guest at the court of King Alfred the Great in England, when Viking raids upon the English coast were at their peak. Ohthere told about his life as a chieftain in northern Norway and his sea voyages from the Arctic Ocean to Denmark. His story was so new and strange to the English court that it was committed to writing, making it the oldest eyewitness account from Scandinavia. At the time of his travels, sailing ships had only been known in Scandinavia for a few generations and long sea voyages opened up a world of new possibilities. Before the year 900, Scandinavian seafarers would establish colonies on Iceland and the North Atlantic islands, from which they would eventually travel further to Greenland and North America.

Stories of new voyages and lands also echoed around the port of Siraf in the Persian Gulf. For the first time, ships from the Middle East began to sail all the way to China. In Southeast Asia, these journeys transformed the straits between Sumatra, Malaysia, and Java into a new hot spot for trade and cultural exchange. One of the explorers whose name became famous was Captain Abhara, a shepherd from the highlands of Persia who ended as a long-haul captain and navigator between India and China. The experiences he and other travellers came home with gave rise to some of the most original travel accounts known to history, with tales ranging from the accurate to the embellished, which were collected in Siraf and other Persian Gulf ports.

Archaeological finds can also reveal stories of voyages. Such was the case of the Byzantine diplomat, Theodosios, whose letter-seal has been found at Ribe and Tissø in Denmark and at Hedeby in northern Germany. From 840–842, he travelled from Constantinople (modern Istanbul) over the Adriatic Sea to Venice, and onwards to the Frankish or Carolingian court at Trier. The objective of the journey was to gain allies in the Byzantine Empire's fight against Muslim pirates who had

Map 1. The World in the Viking Age:
1 Hålogaland
2 Kaupang
3 Ireland
4 Hedeby
5 Truso
6 Venice
7 Constantinople
8 Aylah
9 Siraf
10 Zanzibar
11 Borobudur
12 Suzhou

invaded Crete. The fact that Theodosios sent messages to a far-off corner of the world, which the Byzantine emperor's court had only learned the existence of some few years earlier, was perhaps due to a small group of Scandinavians who had recently sailed down the Russian river systems to Constantinople – the first known voyage along this route. This new continental by-pass quickly gained great importance in Scandinavia and the Mediterranean, and, of course, in the new realm which emerged along the waterways: Russia.

The voyages of Ohthere, Abhara and Theodosios range over half of the globe, from China to the Persian Gulf, from the Mediterranean to Northern Europe and further to the outer-most Arctic reaches of Scandinavia. Nevertheless, their worlds were so closely connected that they could well have had common acquaintances in the places to which they travelled. Archaeological discoveries in recent years have provided new insight into how seafaring changed the world during the Viking Age. Exactly how a long-haul ship from the Indian Ocean may have appeared in Abhara's time has been revealed after the discovery of a wreck near the Indonesian island of Belitung; a ship, laden with wares from China, went down there just before the middle of the 9th century.[1] New finds from

INTRODUCTION 9

trading centres such as Aylah on the Red Sea, Unguja Ukuu on Zanzibar, or Abhara's homeport of Siraf – towns that developed concurrently – demonstrate the complex cultures which emerged at the nodal points of maritime travel. Traces of industries that produced wares for maritime trade have been found in Chinese cities, and in Istanbul, Turkey, large-scale excavations have uncovered one of Constantinople's harbours, with many wrecks of the ships that made the Byzantine Empire a world power at sea.

The centuries leading up to the year 1000 are widely known as the time in which the ancient empires and their urban cultures dwindled.[2] However, at the same time, new networks were emerging, connecting coastlines all around the world. These changes often reflect tangible connections. When Ohthere traded on his journeys in the North Sea, he encountered Arabic silver coins from the Islamic caliphates like those Abhara would have had in his belt on the way to China, and in Scandinavian trading towns he might see glass beads from the same workshops that supplied Zanzibar. The age when this happened is known across the world by reference to a diversity of ruling dynasties and empires. It was the world of the Frankish and Byzantine emperors, the Abbasid caliphs of Baghdad, and the Tang Dynasty of China. But more than this, it was an age when adventurous seafaring wove land and sea together in new ways. It was the world in the Viking Age.

The world Long before our calendar began, sailing ships had already found their way from the Mediterranean to India. Ships had sailed along most of Europe's coasts since the days of the Roman Empire. By comparison, sailing ships were a rather late development in Scandinavia. For thousands of years, small and large boats had been rowed between coasts, but from the late 8th century onwards, historical sources and archaeological finds suggest that something had occurred which made the open seas navigable.

Sailing ships made it possible to reach other worlds. However, there was a great difference between the world that could be reached by ships in antiquity and that in the Viking Age. During the 8th and 9th centuries, the Islamic territories had expanded from Afghanistan to Spain. Luxury goods flooded into the lands surrounding the Persian Gulf, and for the first time in almost 1,000 years, the Mediterranean was no longer the main centre of maritime trade.[3] At the same time, under the rule of the Tang Dynasty, China turned its attention to the sea, and ports sprang up along its coast. In the 7th century, the Grand Canal was created – which would connect southern China with the Yellow River and Beijing to the north – linking the coastline with the heart of the empire and making seafaring a profitable business.[4] In Europe, the Mediterranean lands' traditional domination of trade and politics had been weakened by wars and unrest. The Frankish (or Carolingian) Empire in the West and the Byzantine Empire in the East began instead to develop relations with the lands around the North and Black Seas.[5]

Beyond the borders of the old empires of the Mediterranean, the Middle East, India and China, sailing ships were often greeted with hostility in many parts of the ancient world. In contrast, by the time of Ohthere, Abhara, and Theodosios, many of these places had become societies producing wares that were in high demand and where traders were welcome. In East Africa, kingdoms were being established and commodities such as gold, slaves and ivory began to be exported from the new coastal towns. On Java and Sumatra, rare items such as camphor and spices were prepared for export. In Scandinavia, production of woollen cloth and high-quality iron became important industries. Gradual improvements in shipbuilding, navigation and geographical knowledge as well as greater confidence at sea made longer and safer voyages possible, also in hard weather and difficult waters.

Seafaring over the open ocean was based on the skills to navigate without landmarks, which required many years' experience at sea. This in turn was based on great investment of time and in materials, whether it was specially selected trees for shipbuilding, high-quality iron for rivets, nails, anchors and chains, hand-woven sailcloth, caulking or rope that must be acquired in large quantities. Why did these investments make sense? Sea voyages did not just give access to trade and riches: warriors, diplomats and pirates all used ships in the play for power. Ships gave emigrating colonists hope for a better life at the same time that they ferried captured slaves into wretchedness. Pilgrims, craftsmen and scholars travelled in search of new knowledge. Others were driven by curiosity, like Ohthere, who sailed to the Arctic Sea of his own volition, "to find out how far the land extended". Seafaring allowed one to go beyond the familiar. It was this diversity that gave new significance to maritime contacts during the Viking Age.

Networks   When sailing away from home, travellers focused on some few, well-known destinations. The world became 'small', connected by routes that had previously been navigated and described. New towns were frequently established at the points where these routes intersected. They often lay in locations where onward travel became difficult or dangerous – where waters changed character, routes merged, large rivers met the sea or where seasonal sea-routes were exchanged for inland pathways.

The preconditions that brought people together at these places did not lie in the hinterland surrounding the towns, but in long voyages over the sea. Ships needed harbours with security for men and materials, and markets with enough goods to fill their cargo holds. It needed to be possible to acquire provisions and carry out repairs, and to stay for a number of months if necessary. Some wares came from far inland after the sailing season had ended. These towns were therefore busy all year round. They might lie at great distances from each other. To those who travelled for trade, it was vital that other traders visited the same ports. For seamen who had travelled for months, it made little difference if the journey was a few days longer if a safe harbour and the best markets were the end result.

Maritime towns – emporia – were rarely the mid-points of a district or a kingdom, but links in a network.[6] They were often composed of modest houses of wood and were seldom noted for their temples, town walls or palaces. Yet they housed an unmistakably urban way of life. Here were market streets with exotic wares and skilled craftsmen, well versed in unusual techniques. Here lived people with acquaintances in faraway towns. Foreign visitors moved freely and many languages could be heard. From a great distance, the sight of all the masts of the sailing ships would indicate that these were unique and special places.

Emporia developed as gathering and distribution centres for the great cargos carried by ships. Many of the objects that filled the hulls had been literally unknown beyond their region before seafaring made them available. Ohthere brought walrus tusks as an exotic gift for the king of England. Just a few years later, the ivory of the Arctic had become a highly desirable commodity, which was worked by artists and craftsmen at many sites around Europe. Heavy goods such as lumber, barrels, stone vessels, mass-produced ceramics or heavy quernstones were transported over long distances that would have been unpractical over land. New economic tools such as coins, weights and measuring systems came into use among travellers who needed to settle deals in a fast and unambiguous manner. Ideas and belief systems also travelled by sea. Mosques began to appear in Africa and India, missionary churches were built in Scandinavia, and Buddhism and Hinduism became popular on Java and Sumatra. Ships did not just satisfy a demand for transport – they changed the rules of the game for the individual seafarer and for their societies.

Viking-Age maritime networks and the towns they encompassed are one of archaeology's great discoveries. They have long been known along the coasts of Northern Europe, where large-scale excavations have provided new information on many important sites. More recently, archaeological finds in the Mediterranean and around the Indian Ocean have uncovered a world that was previously only known from passing references in travel accounts. New techniques give archaeologists the possibility to trace the origin of increasing numbers of artefacts from these emporia and to understand the widespread maritime network that they represent. During the Viking Age, seafaring connected different cultures, allowed the diffusion of widely varying trade goods, and ignited cultural changes across the globe. The exploration of this story is a new voyage of archaeological discovery.

OHTHERE'S WORLD

"Ohthere said to his lord King Alfred that he lived furthest north of all Northmen ... he went north along the coast ... as far north as the furthest point reached by the whale hunters."

Paulus Orosius, *Seven Books of Histories against the Pagans*, Old English translation, late 9th century

Creca land ⁊ be eastan, maroa ralonde is pisle lond. ⁊ be
eastan þæm sint dæla þaþe lu þeon zotan be norþan
eastan maroa ra sindon dala mente sin ⁊ be eastan dala
mente san sindon horizti ⁊ be norþan dala mente san sin
don surpe ⁊ besestan him syrsle be norþan horoti is mæz
þa land ⁊ be norþan mæzþa londe sen mende oþþa beorzas
tusten. besestan rusdenu is þær zarseczes earm þe liþ ymb
utan þæt land brettannia. ⁊ be norþan him is þær þær sesti
þenon hæt ost se ⁊ be eastan him ⁊ be norþan sindon norþ
dene ægþer ze on þæm maran landū ze on þæm izlandum ⁊
be eastan him sindon afdrede ⁊ besuþan hi is ælse mosa
þæhe re ⁊ eald secna sum dæl. norþdene habbad be norþan
him þone ilcan sæs earm þenon hæt ost se ⁊ be eastan
him sindon ostiþalsode ⁊ afrede besuþan ostiþ habbad
be norþan him þone ilcan sæs earm ⁊ pineday ⁊ bursten
dan ⁊ besuþan him sindon hæselđan. bursendan habbad
þone sæs earm besestan him ⁊ sueon be norþan ⁊ be eastan
him sint sermende ⁊ besuþan him surse. sueon habbad
besuþan him þone sæs earm ost ⁊ be eastan him sermside
⁊ be norþan him ofer þaserenne is cuenland. ⁊ besestan nor
þan him sindon scride sinne ⁊ be sestan norþ men.

ohthere sæde his hlaforde ælfrede cyninze þæt he ealra
norþ monna norþ mest bude. he cuæð þæt he bude
on þæm lande norþ seardū wiþþa þæt sæ. he sæde
þeah þæt land sie suiþe lanz norþ þonan. ac hit is eal
peste buton on seapū stopum stycce mælū wiciad sin
nas on huntode on wintra ⁊ on sumera on sisc aþe
be þære sæ he sæde þæt he æt sumum cirre polde
sandian hu lonze þæt land norþ rihte læze oþþe
hpæðer æniz mon be norþan þæm peste bude
þa sor he norþ rihte be þæm lande læt him ealne sez

Hic incipit
Periplus
Ohtheri.

JANET BATELY

Ohthere's voyages

Notes of a meeting between the Norwegian Ohthere and Alfred, king of the West Saxons An unusual and fascinating glimpse into the life of a seafarer in Viking-Age Scandinavia is provided by a set of notes based on information obtained from a Norwegian named Ohthere (Old Norse *Ottar*), during an interview or interviews with Alfred, king of the southern English kingdom of Wessex. These notes, along with a second set relating to a voyage through the Baltic by an Englishman called Wulfstan,[1] owe their survival to an extraordinary set of circumstances. First, that Alfred (d. 899 CE) had succeeded unexpectedly to the throne in 871, on the death of an older brother. He was by inclination a scholar, eager to promote what he saw as the much-needed restoration of wisdom and learning in his land, and attracted many foreigners to his kingdom.[2] Second, that Ohthere's replies to the questions put to him were clearly considered of sufficient interest for details to have been recorded. Third, that the end of the 9th century saw an initiative, promoted by the king, to provide and circulate English renderings of what were seen as key Latin texts.

Amongst these texts was a version of Paulus Orosius's *Seven Books of Histories against the Pagans*, an early 5th-century work which covered not only the history but also the geography of the world as it was then known in the West.[3] The section on the geography of Europe presented a special challenge to its anonymous West-Saxon translator, who made a number of changes to his source's parallel accounts of Europe, north and south of the Danube. Not least he greatly expanded and updated the Latin text's 23-word reference to the former before moving on to the latter, and introduced new material that ends with the naming of Northmen as among the neighbours of the *Sweon*.[4] It is this reference to Northmen that, by the time the oldest surviving copy of the Old English version was made, appears to have prompted a reader with access to Ohthere's report to interpolate at this juncture details of what that particular Northman had "said" to the Anglo-Saxon king:[5]

"Ohthere said to his lord King Alfred that he lived furthest north of all Northmen. He said that he lived in the northern part of the land along the West Sea. He said, however, that the land extends a very long way north from there, but it is all waste, except that in a few places, here and there, *Finnas* camp, engaged in hunting in winter, and in summer in fishing by the sea.

He said that on one occasion he wished to find out how far the land extended northwards, and whether anyone lived to the north of the waste. He then went north along the coast, keeping the waste land always to starboard and the open sea to port for three days. He was then as far north as the furthest point reached by the whale hunters. Then he continued in a northerly direction as far as he could sail in the next three days. At that point the land turned eastward, or the sea into

1. The beginning of Ohthere's report in the Lauderdale MS, folio 8. This is the earliest preserved manuscript of the Old English version of Paulus Orosius' text, also called the Old English *Orosius*, ca 900–925 CE (© The British Library Board, Lauderdale MS, Folio 8 recto [from line 22] Add. 47967).

the land, he did not know which, but he knew that he waited there for a west-northwest wind and then sailed east along the coast as far as he could sail in four days.

There he had then to await a wind from the north, for the land there turned in a southerly direction, or the sea in to the land, he did not know which. Then he sailed from there south along the coast, as far as he could sail in five days.

Then a large river stretched there up into the land. He and his companions turned up into the river, because they dared not sail past it for fear of hostility, as the land was all inhabited on the other side of the river. He had not previously encountered any settled land since he left his own home; but all the way he had waste land to starboard, except for fishermen, wildfowlers, and hunters, and they were all *Finnas*, while the open sea was always to port.

The *Beormas* had cultivated their land very well, but they dared not enter it. However, the territory of the *Terfinnas* was all waste, except where hunters camped, or fishermen, or wildfowlers. The *Beormas* told them many stories,

2. Reconstruction of a chieftain's farm excavated at Borg in the Lofoten islands, northern Norway. The 80 m-long building provided living-quarters for the household together with a byre for livestock (Photo: Kjell Ove Storvik/Lofotr Vikingmuseum, Borg in Lofoten).

both about their own land and about the lands that surrounded them, but he did not know what truth there was in this, as he did not see it for himself. The *Finnas* and the *Beormas*, it seemed to him, spoke virtually the same language.

In addition to reconnoitring the area, he went there chiefly for the *hors-hwælas* ['horse-whales', walrus], because they have very fine bone in their teeth (they brought some of these teeth to the king), while their hide is very good for ship's ropes. This whale [i.e., walrus] is much smaller than other whales, being no more than seven ells long. However, the best whale-hunting is in his own land: they are forty-eight ells long and the biggest fifty ells long; of these he said he and six others[6] killed sixty in two days.

Ohthere was a very prosperous man in terms of those possessions that their wealth consists of, that is, of wild animals. When he visited the king he still had six hundred tame animals – they call them reindeer. Six of these were stall-reindeer – highly prized by the *Finnas*, because they capture the wild reindeer with them.

He was one of the principal men in that land; he had, however, no more than twenty head of cattle and twenty sheep and twenty pigs, and the little he ploughed he ploughed with horses. But their wealth consists mainly of the tribute that the *Finnas* give them. This tribute consists of animal skins and birds' feathers and whale's bone, and ship's ropes made of walrus-hide [lit. 'whale's hide'] or sealskin. Each person pays according to his lineage; the most well-born has to pay fifteen marten's skins and five reindeer's and one bear skin and ten measures of feathers, and a garment made of either bear- or otter's skin, and two ships' ropes. Each has to be sixty ells long; one must be made from walrus-hide, the other from sealskin.

He said that the land of the Northmen was very long and very narrow. All of it that may be grazed or ploughed lies beside the sea, and that, nevertheless, is very rocky, and wild moors [barren uplands] lie to the east and above, along the cultivated land. On the moors *Finnas* dwell and the cultivated land is broadest towards the east [i.e., southern Norway] and always the further north the narrower; towards the east it maybe sixty miles broad or a little broader, and in the middle thirty miles or broader, and towards the north, he said, where it was narrowest, it might be three miles broad to the moorland and the moorland after that in some places as broad as one can cross in two weeks, and in some places as broad as one can cross in six days. Then along the land to the south on the other side of the moorland is *Sweoland*, up to the northern part of the land; and along the northern part of the land the land of the *Cwenas*. Sometimes the *Cwenas* make raids on the Northmen across the moorland, sometimes the Northmen make raids on them, and there are very large freshwater lakes throughout the moors and the *Cwenas* carry their boats over land onto the lakes and from there make raids on the Northmen. They have very small and very light boats.

Ohthere said that the region he lived in is called *Halgoland* [Hålogaland]. He said that no one lived to the north of him. Then in the south of the country there is a *port* [trading-place by sea or river] called *Sciringes healh*. To that place, he said, it was not possible to sail in one month, if one camped at night and each day had a favourable wind. And all the time he must sail along the coast; and to starboard will be first Ireland and then the islands that are between Ireland and this land; then there is this land until he comes to *Sciringes healh* and all the way *Norþweg* [the North Way or Norway] will be to port. South of this place *Sciringes healh* a very great sea penetrates the land. It is broader than anyone can see across and *Gotland* [Jutland] is on the other side and after that *Sillende* [southern Jutland]. This sea extends many hundreds of miles up into the land.

And from *Sciringes healh* he said he sailed in five days to the *port* called 'at the Heaths' [Hedeby], which is located between the Wends and Saxons and *Angol* and is subject to the Danes. When he sailed there from *Sciringes healh*, he had Denmark to port and the open sea to starboard for three days. And then two days before he reached the Heaths he had to starboard *Gotland* and *Sillende* and many islands – in those lands the English lived before they came here to this country – and for two days he had to port the islands that are subject to Denmark."

Commentary The presence of a Norwegian at the court of a king who spent much time during his reign repulsing attacks on his kingdom by 'Danish men' and their allies, must have been far from a common occurrence. However, the notes do not tell us how, when, or why Ohthere came to be there. The opening reference to the king as "his lord" (though possibly no more than the incorporation of a formulaic greeting) suggests he was a welcome visitor, yet we do not even know how the king and he communicated with one another. Although there are occasional words and idioms that reflect Norse usage – such as *horshwæl* for Old Norse *hrosshvalr* ('walrus'), or *hran* for Old Norse *hreinn* ('reindeer') – others are attempts at providing English equivalents for unfamiliar terminology,[7] possibly indicating the presence of an interpreter.

At the same time, what was said must occasionally have been reported incorrectly, misleadingly, or from an English perspective. It cannot be the largest species of whale found off Norway – the blue or the fin whale – of which 60 were killed by a handful of men in two days, but more probably the much smaller pilot whale or even the incorrectly classified walrus.[8] When the cultivated part of Norway is described as broadest *eastewerde*, this follows the Norse practice of describing travel to the south coast of Norway as going 'east'.[9] As for the observation that Ohthere kept "no more than" a few farm animals, and used horses not oxen for the "small" amount of land he had under the plough, this reflects the point of view of his West-Saxon audience.

On the other hand, a number of subjects that one might have expected to be under discussion are not covered at all. We are not told, for instance, the size of Ohthere's household, how his reindeer herds were managed, what kind of boats he sailed or sailed in,[10] and whether he sometimes voyaged in convoy. No details are reported of Norway's system of governance, while, though examples are given of tribute from the *Finnas*, no mention is made of other major sources of Norwegian revenue, such as slaves and fish. However, behind the notes' brief statements there surely lies a series of specific questions put during the Norseman's audience with Alfred, and very likely reflecting the king's special interests and concerns – questions about trade routes and distances, for instance, the political geography of the area, and the Norwegian economy.

Ohthere's background Ohthere's home, we are told, is in Hålogaland, in northern Norway, a province that in the late 9th century was administered by a jarl.[11] However from other details given in the text, it would appear that he had a good knowledge of the geography of the entire country. He claims to be among the foremost men in the land. If this is true, and if the account in *Egil's Saga* of Thorolf Kveldufsson's life in Hålogaland in the time of Harald Fine-hair (ca 859–932) is to be believed, Ohthere's household might have

Map 2. Ohthere's world:
1. Hålogaland
2. Kaupang
3. Birka
4. Staraya Ladoga
5. Truso
6. Aggersborg
7. Ribe
8. Hedeby
9. Dorestad
10. Quentovic
11. York
12. Lindisfarne
13. Inchmarnock
14. Dublin

consisted of as many as 100 people, not counting slaves.[12] The food production from Ohthere's farm would have been by no means sufficient to support more than a handful of these.[13] Hence his dependence on "wild animals" for his wealth, including not just his reindeer but most probably also his share of the *finneskat* or tribute that it seems local landholders were at this time given the right to collect from the *Finnas*.[14] It was this tribute, supplemented by what he could obtain from his own hunting trips and explorations that Ohthere surely took on his voyages south to trade.

Ohthere the seafarer We do not know how Ohthere reached Wessex – maybe crossing the North Sea to Shetland and Orkney, then through the Irish Sea or via the Viking kingdom of York and the Danelaw to southern England; or perhaps sailing down the Norwegian, Danish and Frisian coasts to the English Channel. The notes refer only to two voyages and a standard sailing-route. The first round the North Cape and possibly as far as the Varanger Fjord or Kola Peninsula. The second to the Oslo Fjord area, with an extension

3. Small whetstone of banded slate, 4.8 cm long, brought from Ohthere's home region in northern Norway. Found in Hedeby, Germany, ca 825–1050 CE (Stiftung Schleswig-Holsteinische Landesmuseen Schloss Gottorf, Wikingermuseum Haithabu, Germany).

to Hedeby on the Danish-Frankish border.[15] However, the Norwegian was clearly a seasoned traveller and experienced sailor, motivated primarily by commercial considerations, but at the same time having curiosity powerful enough for him to investigate the limits of the known world. (It is tempting to suppose that what caused him to change course on reaching the North Cape was fear of encountering the terrible whirlpool at the northwestern end of the world that some believed violently dragged in and destroyed ships that approached too near.)[16] His visits to *Sciringes healh* (Sciring's haugh or hale,[17] Kaupang) and the *port* called "at the Heaths" (æt Hæþum, Hedeby) took him to two important trading places in Scandinavia,[18] while the trip to England could well have been for a purpose similar to that of Norwegian Thorgils Boomer, who, according to *Egil's Saga* traded a shipload of stockfish, hides, skins and furs there for wheat, honey, wine and cloth.[19] We can only guess whether Ohthere made King Alfred a gift of the walrus tusks that they "brought" to him, or was merely displaying his wares in the hope of a sale.

However, we cannot rule out the possibility that, like so many other Scandinavian seafarers, he had travelled even more widely. References to Ireland and "the islands between Ireland and Britain" (presumably Orkney and Shetland) indicate knowledge of important sea routes from Norway that Ohthere might well have taken. Hedeby acts as both the end-point of the third sailing route he describes and the reported starting-point of the Baltic voyage by Wulfstan, mentioned above, and may well be due to no more than a convenient 'scissors and paste' merging of material by the interpolator of the two accounts. Who can tell what further information may have been lost as a result?

It is hard to believe that Ohthere, coming as he did from an area with numerous boathouses and highly-skilled boatbuilders, would not have been closely questioned about the current design and manoeuvrability of Scandinavian ships. Alfred certainly took a personal interest in such matters, in 896 commissioning longships to go against bands of Viking raiders based in East Anglia and Northumbria. These new boats were "designed on neither the Frisian nor the Danish model, but as it seemed to [the king] most practical".[20]

With his knowledge of Scandinavia and the far north, and his wealth of experiences as a seafarer, the Norwegian Ohthere must have been an invaluable source of information about the world in the Viking Age.

SØREN M. SINDBÆK

The making of the Viking Age

4. Sherds of a soapstone bowl found at Hedeby, Germany, ca 850–950 CE. Ca 33 cm in diameter (Stiftung Schleswig-Holsteinische Landesmuseen Schloss Gottorf, Wikingermuseum Haithabu, Germany).

Hålogaland, northern Norway, is hardly the first place where one would look for traces of the urban networks of the Early Middle Ages. A coast of rugged islands and fjords, birch forests, mountains and bogland stretching far north of the polar circle, this land sustains only a limited rearing of animals, and, thanks to the warm currents of the Gulf Stream along the coast, patches of cereal farming in the short summers of midnight sun. Yet in the 9th century this was home to a cosmopolitan voyager, Ohthere, who visited King Alfred in Wessex to tell of expeditions north for walrus ivory, and of sailing routes south to the trading towns Kaupang and Hedeby.[1]

Archaeology demonstrates the reality of Ohthere's account of rich Viking-Age farmers with far-flung connections in Arctic Norway. A chieftain's farm with an 80 m-long main house excavated at Borg on Vestvågøy, in the Lofoten islands, is one of the grandest buildings known from Viking-Age Scandinavia. Finds from the site include amber beads from the Baltic region, jewellery of gold and jet from the British Isles, and sherds of Frankish wine pitchers and glass beakers.[2] Many richly furnished Viking-Age burials in the region contain brooches, beads or weapons that were almost certainly manufactured in urban workshops more than 1,000 km further south.[3]

Maritime networks were an essential condition of life in the North. To many Viking-Age Scandinavians the sea was not only an important reservoir of food, and often the road to neighbours and local meeting places, but also a link to basic resources that could not be adequately sourced from the local

environment. In compensation for sparse agricultural potential, Arctic Scandinavia offered products that were prized further south: furs, eider down, reindeer antler and skins, walrus tusk ivory, and, from at least the 11th century, dried cod (stockfish).[4] Ohthere and his like were able, by means of sailing, to bridge different ecologies and societies. When, in the course of the 8th century, vessels propelled by sails were adopted into this network society, the maritime way of life developed into long-range expeditions and open-sea exploration.

The Viking expansion marks a high tide of trade and exploration, piracy, migration and conquest across much of Europe. Chronicles from the late 8th century describe occasional raids by pagan strangers on monasteries along the northern coasts of the British Isles, soon followed by increasingly large and well-organised Scandinavian attacks on the western coasts of the Continent. Another aspect of the expansion was the overseas settlement of Scandinavian farming communities in the northern British Isles and, well before the end of the 9th century, in the North Atlantic Faroe islands and Iceland. Further Scandinavian colonisation took place in Greenland in the 10th century and – briefly around the year 1000 – in Newfoundland.[5] The settlement process is charted by archaeological finds of Scandinavian objects and building types, by place-names and written records, and increasingly by genetic evidence.[6]

The third and crucial aspect of the Viking expansion was trade. Trade was practised in Scandinavian societies, as in most others, as a means of amending shortfalls in individual households, and of acquiring non-local commodities or products of specialised craftsmanship.[7] The role of trade changed, however, with the adoption of sailing ships. Ships afforded the long-distance transport of large cargoes, and called for markets at the destination that had the capacity to absorb such quantities of goods and supply desired commodities in return – and to do both quickly enough for voyages to be completed within a sailing season. Long-distance maritime trade therefore invited the rise of maritime trading towns: emporia.

5. Norwegian stone products were traded across Northern Europe. Whetstone of Eidsborg slate, ca 30 cm long, found at Hedeby, Germany, ca 800–1000 CE (Stiftung Schleswig-Holsteinische Landesmuseen Schloss Gottorf, Wikingermuseum Haithabu, Germany).

6. Hedeby seen from the sea, looking west. The massive, semi-circular ramparts were constructed in the 10th century to protect the waterfront town (Archäologisches Landesamt Schleswig-Holstein, Germany).

Emporia were places where large numbers of sailors convened, sanctioned by local rulers and watched by their reeves. Resident merchant communities provided brokerage, bought surplus stocks and supplied provisions, hosting, and storage year round. The most notable of such sites in Ohthere's time included Ribe, Hedeby, Birka and Kaupang in Scandinavia, Dublin and York in the British Isles, Truso in the Baltic Sea and Staraya Ladoga further east.[8] The emporia were integrated with networks of local fairs and markets, and seasonal gatherings including *thing*-assemblies.[9]

Trade in emporia was facilitated by the introduction of standardised means of exchange, including coinage, scales and weights based on units consistent with Islamic weight systems.[10] Trade goods included products from Frankish industries: weapons, non-ferrous metals, quernstones, glass vessels, and, to judge by finds of barrels and amphorae, probably wine. Small items like beads, glass or silk arrived from more distant sources in the Mediterranean and the Near East, in such substantial numbers that, around the year 800, they out-competed local bead-making workshops.[11] Yet the mainstay of Viking-Age trade was almost certainly foodstuffs and animal products – products which rarely survive and are only now gaining

Map 3. The northern extension of the Gulf Stream leads warm surface water from the equator and contributes to a mild climate along the Atlantic coasts of Northern Europe.

The wealth of goods and materials acquired through long-distance voyages, and found in graves, hoards and settlements in the Viking homelands makes it clear that Scandinavians considered such objects to be important. Yet when considered in detail, much of what was exchanged does not appear particularly valuable. The bulk of the jewellery produced in Ribe, Hedeby or Birka consisted of objects of brass, antler or glass – not aristocratic luxuries, but peasant valuables at most. A remarkable proportion of the products acquired through long-distance exchange were objects associated with women: brooches, beads, keys and locks, and supposedly the chests to go with them. Their abundance begs a question. The value of such goods was almost certainly modest by the standards of real wealth in the Early Middle Ages: land and livestock. Why, then, would they have merited the considerable effort put into obtaining them?[16]

Durable, movable forms of wealth held particular importance as an aspect of social relations. Their elementary attraction was in the ability to preserve personal property, to settle disputes and provide security for kin. Whenever death, feud, alliances or marriage re-assembled families, it transformed personal relationships, but also relations of property. Rights of inheritance were passed on, family land risked being scattered, and women in particular risked being left without means. A major motivation for affluent Scandinavian peasants to engage in long-distance exchange was that products acquired

archaeological focus through the application of isotopic and genetic tracing methods.[12]

The emporia sustained particular forms of craftsmanship. Viking-Age Scandinavia is thus characterised by the introduction of highly standardised copper-alloy ornaments, antler combs and glass beads, a characteristic combination of cheap, often imported, materials and highly competent craftsmanship, which could only have been achieved by craftspeople manufacturing large number of combs as commodities for a market.[13] Trade also changed rural production. Finds attest to extensive rural production of wool textiles, and to an increasing exploitation of outland resources, including iron extracted from bog ore, or quarried products such as soapstone pots or whetstones.[14] The value of outland products as commodities is also attested by Ohthere's statement that his most important income was the tribute that he received from *Finnas* in skins of marten, reindeer, bear and otter, birds' feathers, walrus tusks, and ships' ropes made of walrus-hide or sealskin.[15]

in this way could alleviate controversial issues of their social networks.[17]

The kind of interactions that constituted the maritime network of Viking-Age Scandinavia had little regard for regions or distances – although fragile and infrequent they were none the less significant links with urban centres. Ohthere's Hålogaland was as 'urban' as the hinterlands of emporia. Urban trade suffused maritime networks. The nautical skills, knowledge, technology, and the desire that mark the Viking expansion, emerged through generations of long-distance ventures to distant markets, in search of things that would reset political economies and family histories across Scandinavia.

7. Copper alloy brooches, bracelets and glass beads exemplify the refined crafts practised in northern emporia. Ornaments from a woman's grave at Skalleberg, near Kaupang, Norway, ca 800–900 CE (Photo: Eirik Irgens Johnsen, Museum of Cultural History, University of Oslo).

ANTON ENGLERT

Scandinavian ships and seafaring

Ohthere's report to King Alfred of Wessex is the earliest known description of Scandinavian seafaring by one of its inhabitants. Aside from the details he relates about life in the North, his account also illustrates how the introduction of the sail in Scandinavia led to a network of long-distance sailing routes in the Viking Age.

The clinker-built Nordic ship and the introduction of the sail in Scandinavia What kind of vessel would Ohthere have used to carry out his voyages? Given Ohthere's apparent status as an important landowner, who was also engaged in trade, it is most likely that he used his own vessel, possibly the same one for all routes.

Scandinavian boats and ships of the Viking Age were 'clinker-built': with double-ended hulls consisting of a keel with curved stems at either end to which were fastened strakes of overlapping planks, riveted together with iron nails and roves. The iron rivets in combination with wool laid between the planks provided a watertight hull that was reinforced by a complex system of transverse framing timbers in regular intervals. Fastening planks with iron rivets instead of treenails or simple iron nails and using decorative mouldings along the edges of planks and timbers are typical of the Nordic clinker-building tradition which can be traced back to the late Roman Period.

Despite the widespread mercantile and military use of the sail in the Roman Empire, including Britain, the Rhine and the southern North Sea coast, the sail was introduced comparatively late in Scandinavia. The remains of the three oldest known clinker-built boats and ships from the Nydam bog in southern Jutland, sacrificed between the early 3rd and the middle of the 4th centuries, show no trace of sails but were propelled by oars only.[1]

The first iconographic evidence for the use of sails in Scandinavia appears on picture stones on Gotland, dating to the 7th–9th centuries. It is unknown when exactly the sail was adopted in Scandinavia after 600. As late as ca 770 a large, sea-going rowing ship was built in western Norway, known from the burial find of Storhaug on the island of Karmøy. The oldest-dated find of a wind-powered vessel in Scandinavia is the ship from the Oseberg burial mound near Oslo Fjord, built around 820.[2] However, the notorious early Viking attack on the English island of Lindisfarne in 793 and subsequent expeditions to the coasts of Britain and Ireland would have been impossible without the use of sails on the open sea.

Why did the mast and sail came so late to Scandinavia, as they must have been known to at least some Scandinavians who returned from service or other activities abroad in the Roman and Byzantine spheres? At first, the installation of this expensive and conspicuous new technology may have offered little improvement to traditional rowing activities such as local fishing and short-distance travel and raids along the Scandinavian coasts.[3] However, once mast and sail were mastered by Scandinavian seafarers like Ohthere, their range of action increased to such an extent that they made a name for themselves along the coasts and rivers of eastern and western Europe. Whether they tried their luck as raiders or traders, those daring seafarers brought material and cultural wealth back home, opening up international trade and laying the ground for urban settlements and the concentration of political and religious power in Scandinavia. There can be little doubt that the adoption of the sail in Scandinavia and the beginning of the Viking Age as an era in European history are related.

Ohthere's vessel The contemporary ship-finds of Gokstad and Tune from the Oslo Fjord region are the best examples for a large sea-going ship-

8. Planks on a clinker-built boat. Modern reconstruction of a Viking-Age longship at the Viking Ship Museum, Roskilde, Denmark (Photo: Werner Karrasch © Viking Ship Museum in Roskilde).

9. The wide-spread use of iron nails and rivets is typical of the Nordic boatbuilding tradition. A large ship requires ca 250 kg of iron for nails, rivets and roves. Ten tons of bog iron ore and 15 tons of charcoal are needed to produce this amount of iron. Iron rivets and semi-finished roves for building and repairing clinker-built boats. Found at Truso, Poland, ca 800–950 CE (Photo: Leszek Okoński, Collection of the Museum of Archaeology and History in Elbląg, photo archive).

10. The Gotlandic picture stone När Rikvide (left) is one of the earliest depictions of a sailing vessel in the North. Another picture stone from Stenkyrka Lillbjärs III (right), dated to later than 750 CE, shows a more developed vessel (after Lindqvist et al. 1941: figs 466, 512).

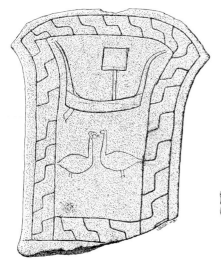

type that Ohthere may have known and used.⁴ Their hulls were mainly built of oak. In Ohthere's home region, far north of where oak can grow, pine would have been used instead. These combined sailing and rowing vessels were ideal for the transport of a large number of people, their travel equipment and cargo. Ohthere could have manned a vessel like the Gokstad ship with able-bodied members of his family, household and retinue. In an age where peace was a matter of local negotiation, a large armed rowing crew was essential to deter pirates and other enemies at sea and ashore. Provided they had enough fresh water and provisions, 30 to 40 men could stay at sea for many days.

Natural conditions of seafaring in Scandinavia

In light of high medieval sources such as the Norwegian *King's Mirror*, it is safe to assume that most voyages took place within the Nordic sailing season from April to September:

"Most seas, apart from the largest ones, one can dare to navigate from the beginning of April. [...] Hardly one should dare an ocean voyage later than the beginning of October, since then the seas become very restless and the storms on them keep growing, the longer fall passes by and winter comes near."⁵

From May to early August, daylight lasts longer than 15 hours everywhere in Scandinavia. In Ohthere's home region of Hålogaland the sun remains above the horizon from 21 May to 23 July.

Wind from favourable directions was the most important natural factor for Viking-Age seafaring, since the use of oars against headwinds was only efficient in calm weather. The details of Ohthere's exploratory voyage to the North and the speed of his voyage from *Sciringes healh* (identified as Kaupang) to Hedeby indicate that he and his contemporaries would wait for fair wind and then sail through long summer days and short summer nights, if their navigational knowledge of the coastal waters permitted it.

Ohthere's network of sailing routes

Ohthere's travelogue pro-vides details of three sailing routes: an exploring voyage from his home in Hålogaland round the North Cape, the route from Hålogaland down the Norwegian coast to a place called *Sciringes healh*, and a third route describing a voyage from Kaupang to Hedeby. Together they cover the entire distance from the south coast of the Kola Peninsula around the North Cape, along the entire coast of Norway and through the Danish archipelago to Hedeby, totalling some 2,200 nautical miles or 4,000 km.

The first and the last routes are reported as individual voyages. The 15-day voyage of discovery to the "northern end of the land" cannot be located with certainty.[6] From a geographical as well as from a nautical point of view, it is likely that Ohthere reached around the Kola Peninsula as far as the Varzuga river.[7]

The second route from Hålogaland to Kaupang is described as a standard route, including directions for Ireland. The length of this route along the "North Way", which gave the country of Norway its name, is indicated by a minimum number of standardised day-sailing distances: it took at least 28 days' sailing if one camped ashore every night instead of sailing on.

Ohthere's last-mentioned, fast voyage of five days from Kaupang to Hedeby must have taken place under favourable conditions of wind and visibility. There is no indication that Ohthere camped at night on this route.[8]

The vast geographical extent of these voyages can be supplemented with two other important travelogues related to the Baltic Sea. Along with Ohthere's report, Paulus Orosius' *Seven Books of Histories against the Pagans* contains a report by Wulfstan on a seven-day voyage from Hedeby to Truso at the mouth of the Vistula.[9] Rimbert mentions in his hagiography of St. Ansgar his dangerous missions to Hedeby and Birka in the mid 9th century, where Ansgar's ship was raided by pirates.[10]

For us today, Ohthere stands out as a vivid example of a maritime businessman in the Viking Age with a widespread overseas network based on his capacity to harvest the Northern Sea for precious animals and to extort his cattle-keeping neighbours. His voyages provide us with rare textual traces of maritime transport and exchange in 9th-century Scandinavia.

11. The Oseberg ship, built around 820 CE in southern Norway, is the earliest archaeological example of a ship with a sail in Scandinavia (Museum of Cultural History, University of Oslo).

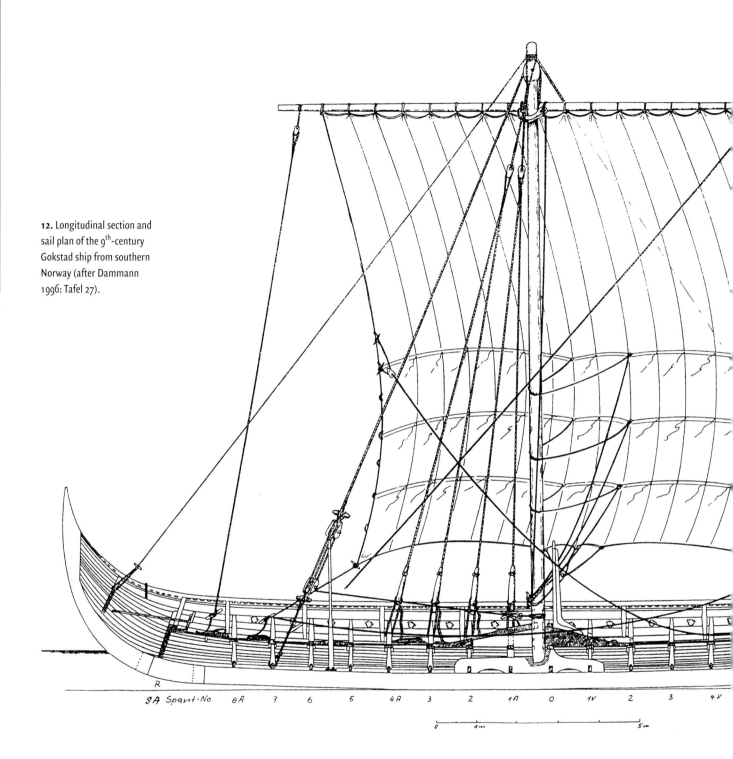

12. Longitudinal section and sail plan of the 9th-century Gokstad ship from southern Norway (after Dammann 1996: Tafel 27).

ANTON ENGLERT

Opening up the Northern Seas: the Gokstad ship

The Gokstad ship is the best preserved example of the nautical technology known in Scandinavia in Ohthere's time. The oak timber for the ship was felled during the last decade of the 9th century, making the ship contemporary with Ohthere's report to King Alfred.[1] The vessel was found in 1880 in the large burial mound of Gokstad near Sandefjord in western Oslo Fjord, Norway. Its deck carried the grave chamber of a chieftain and further splendid grave goods such as three boats, 12 horses and six dogs.[2] The Gokstad ship and its high-status equipment show how Ohthere may have travelled and what kind of material culture may have been at his disposal.[3]

The 23.3 m-long and 5.2 m-wide clinker-built hull provided sufficient buoyancy to support a large single square sail rig of about 120 m². Alternatively, the crew could make use of 32 oar ports in the sides for rowing. Whereas most parts of the ship were made of oak, the deck and the mast and spars for the rigging were made of pine. A single rudder mounted on the starboard quarter was used to steer. The Gokstad ship is fully decked, providing space for the crew to rest and sleep, but without thwarts for the rowers to sit upon. Chests found in the similarly-built Oseberg ship of ca 820 CE[4] and in the harbour at Hedeby[5] suggest that the crew members brought their own sea chests along with them – as seats for rowing and for storing personal belongings. With a maximum draught of 1.2 m,[6] the Gokstad ship was a large and stable vessel that could sail long distances offshore and at the same time reach shallow inshore destinations in fjords and rivers. In 1893, shortly after its excavation, a Norwegian reconstruction of the ship, Viking, proved the seaworthiness of the original design by crossing the Atlantic from Bergen to Newfoundland. Despite a number of strong headwinds, the passage was made in 28 days, averaging a travel speed of 76 nautical miles (141 km) a day.[7]

The 1893 trial voyage indicates that the Gokstad ship had an unlimited operational range in the North Atlantic and along the coasts and rivers of Europe. Fully equipped, the ship could hold an armed rowing crew of 40, their provisions and about 10 tons of cargo or war booty below its loose deck. Therefore, the Gokstad ship can be interpreted as a general purpose vessel for trade and warfare[8] in an age where a seafaring chieftain like Ohthere could engage in the collection of tribute as well as in merchant voyages, depending on his destination and the extent of his power.

About one century later in Scandinavia there was a change towards purpose-built, wider and pure sailing ships for cargo transport and slender longships for troop transport.[9] These types can be seen at the Viking Ship Museum in Roskilde, Denmark. Whereas Ohthere collected and exchanged luxury goods, his successors could specialise in trade, sail bulk cargo and optimise their profit, provided that powerful and benevolent rulers pacified the seas and its trade routes.

SARAH CROIX

The loom and the sail

The introduction of the sail in Scandinavia some time before the year 800 enabled ships to harness the natural strength of the wind and sail farther using less manpower.[1] At the same time, equipping a ship with a sail was an enormous investment requiring massive resources and a large workforce.

While no wool sail has yet been found in archaeological contexts in Northern Europe, the preserved tools required for its fabrication allow us to understand how sails were made. As in Western Europe at the time, textile production was primarily a woman's activity, and these tools are frequently found among the grave-goods in female burials. Textile tools are also frequent finds in Scandinavian Viking-Age settlements. Spindle-whorls and loom-weights are particularly common: made of clay or stone, they preserve very well in most archaeological contexts.

Experiments allow us to reconstruct the quality of sail fabric and assess the time and resources involved. The size of the square sail varied according to the size of the ship: an estimated ca 112–120 m² sail would be required for a 30 m-long longship, representing the wool of ca 200 sheep.[2] The wool was sorted, washed, and combed; it was then hand-spun using a ca 15–20 cm-long spindle, which was weighted down by a spindle-whorl. Weaving

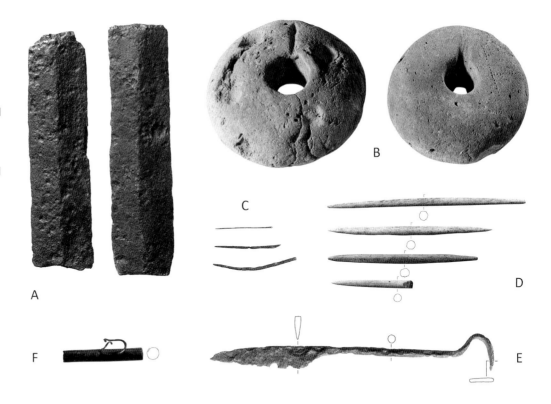

13. Wool textiles, including sail fabric, were produced in quantity on Scandinavian farms. Spindle-whorls, ca 4 cm in diameter, from Aggersborg, Denmark, ca 800–975 CE (Dept. of Medieval and Renaissance Archaeology, Aarhus University).

14. Textile production involved a range of skills and tools. Fragments of iron weaving swords (A), clay loom weights (B), sewing needles of iron and copper alloy (C), bone pin-beaters (D), blade shears (length 17.8 cm) (E), and a copper alloy needle case (F), from Aggersborg, Denmark, ca 800–975 CE. All objects to same scale (Dept. of Medieval and Renaissance Archaeology, Aarhus University).

was performed on a vertical loom (or warp-weighted loom) on which warp threads were hung vertically between the cloth-beam and loom-weights. The weave was made tighter by beating the weft upwards using weaving-swords of iron, wood or whalebone, and was adjusted using a small pin-beater or a comb. The vertical lengths of cloth produced on a loom could then be sewn to each other to form a sail.

Contrary to some other crafts, textile production does not appear to have developed into a specialised intensive production in the first Scandinavian towns.[3] Instead, it essentially took place in the countryside where it required a high degree of organisation in order to connect shepherds, sail-makers and boatbuilders. A chieftain preparing an expedition may have collected cloth produced on the farms of his estate as a type of tax, presented to him in the form of "gifts", or when he enforced dependent workers to gather seasonally at his manor. This is probably the situation reflected in the finds from Aggersborg, Denmark, where hundreds of sunken-featured buildings attest to seasonal activities involving fishing and various productions.[4] Among them would have been the manufacture of textiles of various qualities, including sail cloth.

Considering how time- and resource-consuming the production of cloth was, it is likely that most women were involved in this trade, which does not mean that they all stood on the same footing. Authority was required to gather and organise such large work-forces and, at least at the farmsteads, it was probably the lady of the household who supervised their work. Perhaps it was these ladies who, at the moment of their death, were richly buried with jewellery, household goods and sacrificed animals, along with the textile tools that symbolised their responsibilities.

DRIES TYS

The Low Countries and the Northern Seas

The Low Countries of northwestern Europe in the early medieval period occupied a crucial position as a hinge between the advanced production and rich elites of the Frankish Kingdom and the maritime realms of the Baltic and the North Sea. In the 7th, 8th and 9th centuries, the inhabitants of this region were maritime actors in the exchange of goods and ideas from the different corners of Europe. Ohthere would have encountered them in the large ports of trade in the river deltas of the Rhine, Meuse and Schelde.[1]

The trade centre of Dorestad near Utrecht in the Netherlands is the most important of these early port towns. Between the late 7th and the middle of the 9th centuries, Dorestad became probably the most extensive, well-developed and intensively populated trade port of the contemporary northern world.[2] It was a hub in the early medieval trade network that connected Scandinavia with Gaul and the British Isles with Central Europe. Dorestad comprised at least dozens if not hundreds of jetties for ships to dock. The range of goods traded included prestigious small scale ornamental objects (coloured glass, tesserae for mosaics, amber, silver and gold ingots) to bulk commodities like amphorae and quernstones from the Mayen region in the Rhineland. Wine was traded extensively to other centres along the North Sea, likely in the so-called Reliefband amphorae or in large wooden barrels.[3]

Centres like Dorestad as well as Quentovic in northern France, among others, are regarded as the first new towns in Northern Europe after the fall of the Roman Empire. None of these new towns succeeded Roman town sites, with the exception of Cologne on the Rhine. They instead seem to have been connected with networks controlled by the aristocracy and royalty of the 8th and 9th centuries. Research has long focussed on luxury items, interpreting the emporia as centres of elite gift-exchange, where the aristocracy

15. Quernstones made from basalt quarried near Mayen, Germany. Diameter 47 cm. Found at Aggersborg, Denmark, ca 800–975 CE (Moesgaard fotolab).

16. Ceramic vessel ('Reliefband amphora') for transport and storage. Produced in workshops near Cologne, Germany. Height 53 cm. Found in Emden, the Netherlands, ca 900 CE (The Frisian Society for History and Culture/Fries Museum, Leeuwarden, The Netherlands).

17. Wine barrel made from oak, probably from the Moselle region, Germany. Height 1.8 m. Found at Jelsum, the Netherlands, ca 750 CE (The Frisian Society for History and Culture/Fries Museum, Leeuwarden, The Netherlands).

controlled the social and political distribution of these prestigious items. Today, it is clear that large quantities of everyday bulk goods were also traded here. The trade of quernstones, lead, copper alloys, antler combs, wool and woollen cloth, raw iron and ceramics in the North Sea basin and beyond shows a vibrant economy of production and exchange – much less self-sufficient than researchers once believed.[4]

New archaeological research has shown that the network of the production and trade settlements was more complex than previously understood, and many more people had access to luxurious commodities. Imported and/or luxury goods that were once thought to occur only in the large new ports also appear at rural sites in the Low Countries, British Isles and Scandinavia. A range of large and small private and public markets and local trade centres existed in between the large ports, ranging from coastal free farmers' settlements, aristocratic and non-aristocratic rural estates to smaller ports, for instance near abbeys with craft production.[5]

The network of these new northwestern European urban centres in the 8th and 9th centuries in the North Sea basin was also connected to the trade of human 'goods' – slaves – exchanged especially for silver, but also other commodities originating from the Byzantine and Islamic lands in the Mediterranean and Near East.[6] We may ask indeed if this input of silver bullion by the contemporaries of Ohthere was an important stimulus to the development of exchange in crafted and bulk products in the Frankish Low Countries.

STEVEN P. ASHBY
& ASHLEY COUTU

Arctic resources and urban networks

Ohthere's journeys linked his homeland in northern Norway to trading towns more than 1,000 km to the south. New archaeological data are beginning to trace the connections between the Arctic North and southern urban markets. The evidence comes from the animals that made up a substantial part of Ohthere's wealth: reindeer.[1] Antler from deer was an invaluable product in pre-modern craft and industry. In the early medieval period, this raw material was used to produce of a range of valued items including hair combs. As a result, it began to be exploited on a previously unprecedented scale.[2]

A rich assemblage of antler hair combs and waste from the workshops that made them has been excavated in the emporium of Ribe on the southwest coast of Jutland in Denmark.[3] Using a recently developed biomolecular technique, the species of antler used here can be identified.[4] A study of some 200 samples, covering the period ca 700–860 CE, has shown that most material from the early phases belongs to species which occurred locally in Jutland: red and roe deer. However, from about 780, fragments of reindeer antler occur both among the workshop debris and in finished combs. Even from much earlier, before ca 725, a few fragments from finely decorated combs of reindeer antler are found. As reindeer antler was only a small fraction of the material worked by combmakers in Ribe at this time, these combs were most likely produced in Norway and arrived as the personal possession of a Norwegian visitor to the site.

The reindeer antler from Ribe is the earliest product from Norway so far identified in trading towns in the south, but this was soon followed by other commodities: whetstones of slate, soapstone bowls, and walrus ivory – items acquired from special quarries or from Arctic hunting grounds. Walrus ivory, which Ohthere brought to King Alfred, soon became a highly-sought luxury good, and may have been partly what attracted Scandinavians to explore the North Atlantic and settle in Iceland and Greenland.[5]

18. Fragment of a comb found in Ribe, Denmark, ca 10 cm long, made from Norwegian reindeer antler, ca 725–850 CE (Museums of Southwest Jutland, Denmark).

19. Fragments of reindeer antler, imported from Norway to Hedeby, Germany, as a raw material for urban craftsmen, ca 825–1050 CE (Stiftung Schleswig-Holsteinische Landesmuseen Schloss Gottorf, Wikingermuseum Haithabu, Germany).

The fact that reindeer antler appears in quantity in Ribe at the same time as oriental beads and coins first began to find their way to Scandinavian emporia, and shortly before chroniclers record the earliest Viking raids in the British Isles and Western Europe, implies that urban networks were swiftly developing, and were a key component in the build-up of the maritime culture, technology and know-how that led to the Viking expansion, and linked the far north with the world beyond.

ABHARA'S WORLD

"Then he became a captain, and sailed the sea in all directions. He went to China seven times. Only adventurous men had made this voyage before."

Buzurg Ibn Shahriyar, Captain Abhara's story in *The Marvels of the Wonders of India*, 10th century

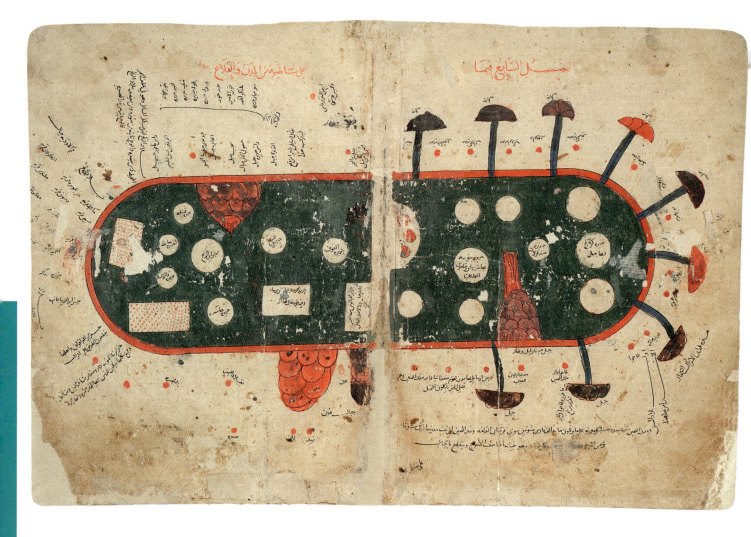

DIONISIUS A. AGIUS[1]

Abhara's voyages

The Marvels of the Wonders of India: Mainland, Sea and Islands (Kitab 'aja'ib al-Hind, barruhu wa bahruhu wa-jaza'iruhu in Arabic) is a collection of sea stories compiled by the sea captain, Buzurg Ibn Shahriyar al-Ramhormuzi towards the mid to late 10th century. They contain details of life at sea in the Indian Ocean world, especially its dangers, shipwrecks, long-distance sea trade, strange creatures, magic, superstition and belief. In addition to their literary value, for the modern researcher the stories are a source of information about types of water craft, nautical skills, star navigation, and knowledge of winds and currents.

The book's 136 sea stories were set at a time when maritime trade in the Indian Ocean in the 9th and 10th centuries was flourishing, and perilous voyages were made from the Persian Gulf to the southwest coast of India, the east coast of Africa, the islands of Java and Sumatra, and China. These stories, written in Arabic, have touches of fantasy but are mixed with facts.

20. Many of the places named in Buzurg Ibn Shahriyar's book *The Marvels of the Wonders of India* are also noted on a map of the Indian Ocean in the Arabic treatise *The Book of Curiosities of the Sciences and Marvels for the Eyes*, compiled in Egypt or Greater Syria in the late 12th or early 13th centuries, based on a work made in Egypt before ca 1050 CE. Around the oval-shaped green sea are names of cities, peoples and geographic features like mountains (the mushroom-like shapes on the right). The left side of the map, from top-centre to bottom-centre, describes from Cape Guardafui in Somalia south along the East African coast and back up to Aden in Yemen, listing "the land of the Zanj", "islands of the Waqwaq", and the Maldives. In the sea near the bottom is a white rectangle oriented length-wise in which is the description: "The Island of Unjuwa [Zanzibar]. There are twenty (?) anchorages around it. It has a town called Ukuh (?) [Unguja Ukuu?]". The right side of the map, from top-centre to bottom-centre, describes the west coast of India, the mouth of the Indus, to cities in China, listing "Tahu [= Khanju], the seat of the ruler of China. On land, it is 300 farsakhs from Khafur [Khanfu? – probably Guangzhou in southern China] ...". At the bottom in the sea is "... a mountain in which there is fire night and day" – probably a volcano somewhere in the Indonesian archipelago (The Bodleian Libraries, University of Oxford. MS. Arab. C. 90, fol. 29b–30a: Book 2, Chapter 7).

Buzurg was a Persian from Ramhurmuz, a town in the province of Khuzistan, in southwest Persia. He compiled his collection at the height of shipping activity in the Indian Ocean. From the stories, it is possible to deduce that he was an experienced sea captain, who had probably settled in Siraf, on the eastern shore of the Persian Gulf, in present-day Iran.[2]

Buzurg's dynamic collection of sea stories are often narrated with a touch of humour and with an element of exaggeration for effect. They portray the lives of mariners and their heroism on land and at sea, giving a wealth of information on the traditions of the coastal peoples, their beliefs and superstitions. A common theme is of seafarers surviving storms and shipwrecks.

One of "the stories told about sailors and captains" is that of Captain Abhara, an extraordinary sea captain, who sailed to China seven times, probably in the 9th century. Such voyages were dangerous, as many people lost their lives and it was a miracle to return safe and sound. Abhara experienced shipwrecks and other calamities but he accomplished the remarkable feat of returning without mishap to Siraf. This is his story, narrated to Buzurg by another captain, called Shahriyari:

Captain Abhara's story[3]

[Buzurg Ibn Shahriyar recounts]: Amongst the stories told about sailors and captains, here is one about Captain Abhara. He was a native of Kirman [in present-day southeast Iran], where he was a shepherd in the desert. Then he became a fisherman, and then a sailor on a ship that went to India. Next he was on a Chinaman. Then he became a captain, and sailed the sea in all directions. He went to China seven times. Only adventurous men had made this voyage before. No one had done it without an accident. If a man reached China without dying on the way, it was already a miracle. Returning safe and sound was unheard of. I have never heard tell of anyone, except him, who had made the two voyages there and back without mishap.

It happened to Abhara that he was adrift in his ship's boat with a skinful of water, and so remained for several days. This is what Captain Shahriyari, one of the sea captains on the China route, said:

"I was going from Siraf to China. When I was between Sanf [on the coast of Vietnam], and China near Sandal-Fulat, at the end of Sanji which is the Sea of China, all of a sudden the wind fell and we had a flat calm. We anchored, and stayed still for two days. On the third day we saw something far away on the sea. I lowered the ship's boat, and four sailors embarked with orders to identify the black object. They went and returned.

'Well?' I said. 'It is Captain Abhara, in his ship's boat, with a skin of water.'

'Why have you not brought him here?' I asked.

'We wanted to do so', they said. 'But he answered, saying:'

'I will only come aboard your ship as captain with full powers. My salary

21. Siraf was a cosmopolitan port and the wealth brought to it by trade made it possible for its population to buy imported luxury goods such as jewellery and decorate their houses lavishly. Silver ring about 2 cm in diameter, with an illegible Arabic inscription, Siraf, Iran, ca 800–1000 CE (© Trustees of the British Museum).

will be a thousand *dinars* in merchandise at the market rate in Siraf.'

We were astounded by his words. Together with some sailors I went and saw him on the water, rising up and down with the sea. We greeted him to come with us. He said:

'Your situation is worse than mine. I am in less danger than you. I will come on board, if you give me a thousand *dinars* worth of merchandise at the Siraf rate and give me command of the ship.'

We said:

'The ship has much merchandise and considerable wealth on board, and very many people. It would do us no harm to have Abhara's advice for a thousand *dinars*.'

So he embarked, with his waterskin and his ship's boat. Hardly had he arrived than he said:

'Give me the thousand *dinars* worth of merchandise.'

They gave him them. When he had stowed them safely, he said to the captain:

'Go away.'

And the captain went away, and made room for him.

'Now to work', he said. 'We have no time to waste.'

'What are we to do?' we said.

'Throw everything heavy into the sea.'

They threw it overboard, and the ship was lightened of half its cargo, or more.

'Cut down the mainmast', he said:

'Raise the anchors, and let the ship drift.'

We obeyed. He added:

'Cut the cable of the large anchor.'

We cut it, and it fell into the sea. He had the other anchors thrown overboard, and six of them were thrown away. On the third day a cloud like a minaret [waterspout] appeared. It spread out over the sea, and a gale engulfed us. If we had not lightened the ship and cut down the mast, we would have been swamped by the first wave that struck us. The gale went on for three days and three nights. The ship pitched and tossed, without an anchor or a sail. Whither it went we did not know. Next day the wind dropped, and then calmed altogether, and by the end of that day the sea had become calm. By the morning of the fifth day the sea was peaceful, and the wind in our favour. We stepped a jury mast [a makeshift mast] and dressed the sails. The ship sailed on, safely, by God's grace. We reached the Chinese coast. There we repaired the ship, and replaced the mast we had thrown away in the sea. After we had stayed as long as we needed for our sales and purchases, we set sail again, and left China for

Siraf. When we reached where we reckoned we had found Abhara, we remembered an island and some rocks.

'Anchor', said Abhara.

This done, we lowered the ship's boat, and fifteen men got in it.

'Go over there', he said, 'and pick up the anchor you find there.'

These words surprised us, but no one wanted to contradict him. We obeyed, and the sailors found the anchor, and brought it back. Then he said:

'Go to that rock over there, and pick up such-and-such an anchor.'

This was done. Then he ordered:

'Raise the yards.'

We carried the order out, and the ship resumed its course. We questioned Abhara about the anchors.

'When I met you', he said, 'it was at the high tide of the thirtieth day, but it had already gone down a lot. Your ship was sailing between those rocks and this island. I made you throw the heaviest of your cargo overboard. After that I thought about the anchors. We had no particular need for them in China, and the merchandise still on board weighed at least double these anchors. I made you jettison them because it was absolutely essential to lighten the ship. Three out of the six remained visible on the reefs and on the island, the other three went to the bottom.'

'How', they asked him, 'could you foresee the way the water went down and the gale?'

'I, and others before me', he said, 'have already crossed that sea. We have observed that on each thirtieth day the water goes down in an extraordinary way, so as to leave these rocks bare. At the same time a violent gale rose from the deep. The ship I was in was wrecked on one of these rocks, because low water occurred while we were spending the night above the reef, and I escaped in this ship's boat. If you had stayed where I met you, your ship would have grounded in less than an hour, before the gale occurred, because you were above the island, and, if it had struck those rocks, it would have broken in pieces'."

This Abhara had much sailing experience, and many stories about it. This was one of the best.

The story and its context Earlier than Buzurg's collection of sea stories, we have Arabic works which contain, amongst other stories, some descriptions of sea voyages and events of the landscape and seascape of the Indian Ocean, later recorded by historians and geographers.[4] Some descriptions in these early works contain marvels and wonders called 'aja'ib, a genre developed in the early medieval period. Although Buzurg's stories fall within the theme of wonders and marvels, they also offer a wealth of information on diverse subjects that are both instructing and entertaining, touching on the human element of life by and at sea with a moral or message at the end of some stories.

The stories of Buzurg Ibn Shahriyar, however, are also one of the earliest examples of exclusively maritime literature. They are unique in that no collection of sea stories, with the exception of the "Seven Voyages of Sindbad the Sailor" in the *Arabian Nights*, has ever appeared up to modern times. The first time Sindbad's seafaring stories appeared in the west was through Antoine Galland's (d. 1715) French translation of the *Arabian Nights*,[5] based on an Arabic manuscript from the 1690s. But the story-cycle of Sindbad's voyages probably goes back to the early medieval period and possibly further, to Persian (Pahlavi) or Indian (Sanskrit) origins, though influences of Greek mythology[6] are clearly evident and this comes as no surprise as stories, like trade goods, travel with merchants and mariners through the desert and over the sea. Hence Buzurg Ibn Shahriyar may well have come across the popular stories of Sindbad the Sailor.

As in the story of Abhara, many of Buzurg's sea stories are about Siraf, its mariners and merchants, activity to and from China and the ports of the western Indian Ocean,[7] including tales about East Africa.[8] Ships setting off from Siraf to China and back became more and more frequent even though the sea voyage was hazardous and often ended in tragedy as several of Buzurg's stories tell and the geographer and historian, al-Mas'udi (d. 956 CE), reports. Although many of the crew and passengers were from Siraf, that did not mean they were Sirafis, or even Persians, as Siraf was a great cosmopolitan port city which attracted sailors and traders from all over the Indian Ocean.[9] There were Arabians, East Africans, Indians, Javanese, Sumatrans and Chinese, to mention a few.

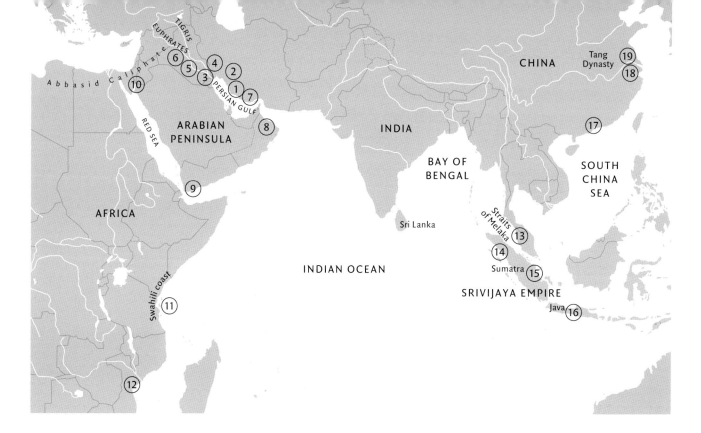

Map 4. Abhara's world:
1 Siraf
2 Shiraz
3 Basra
4 Uballah
5 Kufa
6 Baghdad
7 Kish
8 Sohar
9 Aden
10 Aylah
11 Zanzibar
12 Sofala
13 Kedah
14 Barus
15 Palembang
16 Borobudur
17 Guangzhou
18 Suzhou
19 Yangzhou

The core of the story of Abhara is the voyage from Siraf to China and its perils. Its dramatic effect comes from the description of the gale and the resulting shipwreck. Here the story is not so much embellished with marvels and wonders as are the others; rather it seems to be describing actual realities. The main character, Abhara is a remarkable man: from humble beginnings he became a *rubbān* (a captain and navigator), who knew how to steer a ship in fair and rough winds and above all could navigate close to coastal areas; he had even navigated a "Chinaman" (*markab ṣīnī*). We know that he had sailed to China many times on trading voyages and the remarkable skills he had acquired are the focus of this story, enabling him to save Captain Shahriyari's ship and crew.

All these details would be fascinating to an audience of sailors. There is a touch of humour in the way that Abhara negotiates a very hard bargain with Captain Shahriyari and the sailors, offering his services for 1,000 *dinars* "worth of merchandise at the Sirafi rate", which they agreed upon as the ship had "much merchandise and considerable wealth on board". The point the narrator is making here is the astuteness of Abhara, something his mercantile audience would appreciate, but for the modern reader it offers an intriguing insight into trade transactions of the time.[10]

Apart from the "Seven Voyages of Sindbad the Sailor" of the *Arabian Nights*, Buzurg's sea stories are unique in the history of Arabic literature but share parallel themes with other cultures – one of which is the well-known account of *The Odyssey*,[11] attributed to Homer (ca 8th century BCE), where we find similarities with Buzurg's accounts of ships being driven off course and the triumph of nautical skills save the day. Similarly, the apocryphal *Acts of Andrew* (1st century CE) portray scenes of shipwrecks and pirates.[12] These stories circulated among early Nestorian Christians in Asia Minor, reaching the islands of Failaka and Beni Iyas (opposite Abu Dhabi) in the Persian Gulf long before Islam.[13] They may well have influenced the Arabic stories but they may also have arisen independently of each other.

Buzurg's stories are written in the vernacular, thus breaking away from the canon of good Arabic literary style; further proof that they were written for an uneducated audience of sailors and traders. Unlike the *Arabian Nights* which were orally transmitted until they were finally written down, Buzurg's sea stories were first-hand accounts which he wrote down, capturing a moment in time.

These stories about Arabian, Persian and Indian sealore written in Arabic demonstrate a commonality of practices in seafaring and navigation throughout the Indian Ocean. Although several stories speak about Sirafis and their journeys to and from China, there are no details as to the length and frequency of these journeys. It is odd that no Chinese captain or merchant is recorded; there is, however, mention of a Chinese ship in the story of Abhara.

In the absence of information on these matters it is worth considering what the Arabic sources mean when they report about ships sailing to China: do they mean Arabian, Persian or Indian ship-types or Chinese junks? Archaeology has yet to reveal shipwrecks to confirm the details of their type, construction and size – only generalities are known. The 9th-century Belitung shipwreck discovered off the Indonesian coast raises more questions than answers to this historical and archaeological puzzle,[14] but it is for now one of the best possibilities we have for understanding the logistics and realities of Abhara's distant voyages.

22. Houses in Siraf were built using imported wood and decorated with stucco, carved into elaborate patterns. Fragment of a stucco wall decoration with leaf design, ca 17 cm high, Siraf, Iran, ca 800–1100 CE (© Trustees of the British Museum).

TIMOTHY POWER

The Abbasid Indian Ocean trade

23. From the Persian Gulf region, date syrup (*dibbs*) was traded throughout the wider Indian Ocean. Remains of its distinctive packaging containers – ca 40 cm-high turquoise alkaline glazed jars made in southern Iraq – have been found in Zanzibar, Siraf and Aylah (The David Collection, Copenhagen, Denmark. Inv. no. 27/2003).

Persian Gulf trade within the wider Indian Ocean was well established by the time Buzurg Ibn Shahriyar compiled his sea stories in *The Marvels of the Wonders of India*. Yet trade with China was not routine when Buzurg's Captain Abhara swapped his flocks for fleets.[1] Maritime contacts between the Gulf and China were probably established in the mid 8th century, when the Abbasid Dynasty (750–1258 CE) ruled from Iraq and the Tang Dynasty ruled in China (619–907), thus framing the Indian Ocean world between two great empires.[2] An archaeological study of ceramics from the Persian port of Siraf demonstrates that imported Chinese ceramics first appear shortly before ca 750–775.[3] The earliest reasonably well-placed historical instance of a Muslim merchant sailing to China belongs to the mid 8th century, when the Omani captain Abu Ubayda returned with a cargo of aloes wood.[4]

Merchants from the Persian Gulf played a key role in pioneering direct maritime contact between Southwest and Southeast Asia. At the head of the Gulf lie the rich alluvial plains of modern Iraq, stretching out between the Euphrates and Tigris rivers. Archaeological survey of "the land behind Baghdad" suggests that agricultural

46 ABHARA'S WORLD

development peaked under the Sasanians, the imperial Persian dynasty which ruled the region immediately before the coming of Islam.[5] The Muslim conquest of the Euphrates frontier zone, which once separated the warring Byzantine and Sasanian Empires, subsequently created a massive 'free-trade zone'. Under Islam's first dynasty, the Umayyads based in Damascus (661–750), the abundant wealth of Iraq attracted Arab settlers, housed in the newly established cities of Basra and Kufa, which developed into powerful regional markets. By the time the Abbasids came to power in 750, Iraq was arguably the very richest province of their vast empire, and for this reason was chosen as their base of operations.[6] The establishment of a new Abbasid capital on the banks of the Tigris in 762 took full advantage of the global trade already passing through the Persian Gulf. "This is the Tigris," Caliph al-Mansur is recorded as saying when he established Baghdad, "there is no obstacle between us and China; everything on the sea can come to us on it".[7] Demand for luxury goods by the thriving bourgeoisie and imperial court in Iraq therefore helped drive the eastwards expansion of Indian Ocean trade.

During the heyday of the Abbasid Indian Ocean trade, roughly between the mid 8th and mid 9th centuries, Basra was undoubtedly the greatest city of the Persian Gulf.[8] Merchants could sail down the Tigris from Baghdad to Basra, where a canal continued through the marshes of the Shatt al-Arab to the sea port of Uballah, and from there make for the Iranian port of Siraf. The next port of call was Sohar, on the Arabian coast of the Gulf of Muscat, home of the fictional character Sindbad the Sailor. It was from these ports that the ocean-going ships set sail on their epic voyage to China, which a contemporary geographer writes would take at least 120 days.[9] This journey took them past Sri Lanka and Sumatra, eventually to put into the ports of Guangzhou and Yangzhou.[10] In the later 9th and 10th centuries, Siraf and Sohar grew to eclipse Basra and Uballah.[11] By this time Muslim merchants no longer sailed on the South China Sea but rather stopped short at the Straits of Melaka, which the geographer al-Mas'udi, writing in 947, tells us became "a general meeting place for the Muslim vessels of Siraf and Oman and the ships from China".[12]

The range of goods traded between Abbasid Iraq and Tang China remains in some ways mysterious. The Chinese were certainly exporting silk and porcelain, for which there was an almost insatiable demand in Iraq and Iran; as al-Mas'udi wrote of the Chinese: "no other nation can compare with them in any craft whatsoever".[13] But what products of Persian Gulf origin could interest the Chinese? It has often been thought that quantities of date syrup, or *dibbs*, were exported in the turquoise alkaline glazed jars produced in southern Iraq and found throughout the Indian Ocean.[14] Pearls were certainly harvested in the Gulf region during the Abbasid period and may also have been exported to China. The frankincense of southern Oman was quite possibly

24. The foundations of the courtyard of the Congregational Mosque of Siraf, looking over the Persian Gulf. Built in 803–804 CE, the mosque was enlarged over the next several centuries – no doubt due to the growing wealth of the port city's merchant population. At its full extent, the mosque measured 55 × 44 m, and had several cisterns, an absolution area, a minaret and bazaar surrounding it (Photo: Athena Trakadas).

25. Lighting was necessary for every house, shop and mosque of Siraf. Hanging glass lamp, ca 22 cm high, southern Iraq, ca 800–900 CE (The David Collection, Copenhagen, Denmark. Inv. no. 14/1985).

also exported, for aromatics appear amongst the 'tribute' brought by the *Po-ssu*, the Chinese term for Persians and other Southwest Asians.[15] Such commodities may well have contributed to the trade, but it seems rather that the Gulf merchants engaged in the 'country trade', which is to say they undertook to supply China with products from other countries. A good example is ivory. Al-Mas'udi tells us that Indian ivory was used to make the canes carried by all Chinese civil servants and military officers, and that quantities of ivory were burnt as offerings in the Chinese temples, suggesting that there was considerable demand for this commodity.[16]

Although he is silent as to how Indian ivory reached China, one might well imagine that it was being brought there by Muslim merchants as part of a 'country trade'.

The scale and wealth of maritime trade with India and China was the stuff of legend. Wealthy communities of Muslim merchants emerged in the port cities of China, the size of which were considerable if the sources are to be believed. Several thousand Arabs and Persians were said to have been killed in Yangzhou during a rebellion of the year 760, and 120,000 Muslims, Christians, Jews and Zoroastrians were later believed to have been massacred in another revolt in Guangzhou in 878.[17] It was said that the merchants of Basra active in the Indian Ocean trade had an annual income of over a million *dirhams* each, that the average merchants' house in Siraf cost over 10,000 *dirhams*, and that the richest of the Siraf merchants were worth around four million *dirhams*.[18] An immediate impression of the scale of the trade may be gained from the Belitung wreck near Sumatra, where tens of thousands of porcelain and stoneware bowls were retrieved from the skeletal remains of a western Indian Ocean ship.[19] The impact Chinese porcelain and other ceramic imports such as these on the local potteries of Iraq is thought to have informed the origin of distinctively Islamic glazed ceramics, a tradition which was to develop into one of the most characteristic media of Islamic art.[20]

The Abbasid Indian Ocean trade began to decline after the mid 9th century.

Already the Abbasid caliph al-Wathiq (r. 842–847) had been forced to intervene to promote the Indian Ocean trade in Iraq, abolishing import duty and building harbour facilities, the first evidence for state involvement in the trade. Disturbances in Tang China adversely affected the Indian Ocean trade with Abbasid Iraq, particularly the Guangzhou massacre in 878, and in 907 China plunged into a generation of civil war.[21] Similarly, Abbasid rule and Iraqi prosperity were then seriously undermined by violent revolts at home by Turkish slave soldiers (ca 861–870), East African agricultural slaves known as Zanj (ca 868–883), and extremist Shi'a known as the Qarmatians (ca 873–907). The pre-eminent Gulf emporium of Basra was sacked by the Zanj slaves in 871 and again by the Qarmatians in 923. The Abbasid state in Iraq was bankrupt by the time of the accession of the caliph al-Mu'tadid in 892.[22] At the same time, the rise of powerful new dynasties in the Red Sea region began to lure Indian Ocean trade away from the Persian Gulf, a process catalysed by the foundation of Cairo in 969 by the ascendant Fatimid Dynasty.[23] Siraf was laid low by an earthquake in 977, after which time it was eclipsed by Sohar in Oman, for the geographer al-Muqaddasi, writing in 985, states that "in the period of its prosperity, it was superior to Basra … Siraf and not Oman was the transit port of China and the entrepot of Persia".[24] It was therefore towards the twilight of Siraf's golden trading years that Buzurg Ibn Shahriyar began to record the sea captains' stories he heard there, perhaps because it was clear that the maritime culture of Siraf was slowly fading away, and the great days of sailing to China from the Gulf had already passed into legend.

26. Chinese ceramics that were imported to the Persian Gulf inspired local ceramic developments. "Splash ware", manufactured in southern Iraq, imitated Chinese forms like Changsha bowls and also Chinese techniques like tin- and lead-glazing, giving a white finish. This "Splash ware" bowl has green and brown splashes added, with the name "Ubayd" in the middle in blue. Ca 20 cm in diameter, southern Iraq, ca 800–900 CE (The David Collection, Copenhagen, Denmark. Inv. no. 38/2001).

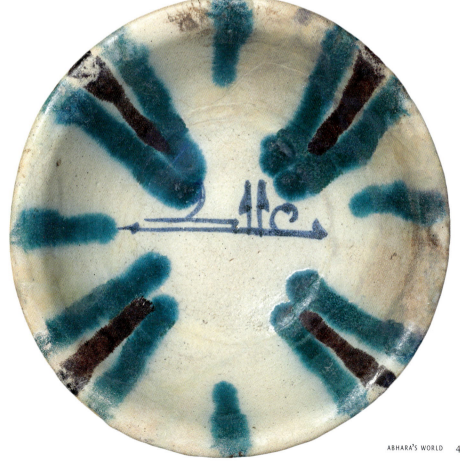

STEPHANIE WYNNE-JONES

Africa's emporia

"The Zanj … settled in that area which stretches as far as Sofala, which is the furthest limit of the land and the end of the voyages made from Oman and Siraf on the sea of Zanj. In the same way that the sea of China ends with the land of Japan, the sea of Zanj ends with the land of Sofala and the Waqwaq, which produces gold and many other wonderful things. It has a warm climate and is fertile …." – al-Mas'udi, *The Golden Meadows and Mines of Gems*[1]

This description by the 10th-century Arab geographer al-Mas'udi of the land of the "Zanj" refers to the region known today as the Swahili coast, which runs approximately 3,000 km from Somalia to Mozambique.[2] Today, the shoreline and islands of Africa's eastern coast are dotted with the remains of coral-built Islamic ports of trade, or emporia, that were and are home to a merchant elite. The grandest monuments – mosques, tombs and palaces – date to the golden age of Swahili trade in the 13th and 14th centuries. Yet, as al-Mas'udi's description above demonstrates, this stretch of coast had long been incorporated into Indian Ocean trade networks and was famed for its export goods across the Islamic world, and onward to markets in India and China.

Coastal sites of the 8th century onwards have evidence for imports of manufactured objects from exotic ports among the locally-produced goods.[3] These included porcelains and glazed ceramics, as well as glass beads; yet the bulk of the trade was probably in commodities that are now hard to trace such as cloth or foodstuffs. The sites were also busy industrial centres, producing iron goods and beads of marine shell, and trading with the African hinterland as well as with overseas merchants from the Persian Gulf, as mentioned by al-Mas'udi, above, and described in several of the tales related by Buzurg Ibn Shahriyar. Perhaps this included Abhara, who allegedly "sailed the sea in all directions".[4] Al-Mas'udi reports that the people of East Africa exported ambergris and resins, leopard skins, tortoise-shell and ivory which was highly prized in the workshops of India and China. To this list we might add commodities mentioned by other Arab geographers contemporary to al-Mas'udi: particularly mangrove wood, gold, and slaves. Archaeologically these exports are all difficult to recognise, although sometimes we see hints preserved. At Manda, an important trading town in northern Kenya, for example, remains of ivory working were encountered during excavations.[5]

The people conducting this trade lived in quite humble settlements. The buildings were all constructed of mud and thatch. During these early centuries they were truly village settlements, with no evidence for hierarchy or for specialisation of production. Even mosques were on a small scale and built in mud and thatch.[6] In later centuries these were replaced by coral-built structures. The process of mosque construction and enlargement also illustrates the growing Islamic

27. Foundations of the 9th-century mosque during excavations at Shanga, Kenya (Photo: Mark Horton).

community on the coast. Although Islam was practised here from the 8th century, introduced through regular contact with the Islamic world rather than through conquest or migration, it was only from the 11th century that Muslims appear to have been in the majority.[7]

In the 8th and 9th centuries, the Swahili people made their living through small-scale agriculture and fishing. Their diet of cattle, sheep, fish and crops such as millet is visible through archaeological excavations at a series of sites occupied during these centuries. One site, Tumbe on Pemba Island off the Tanzanian coast, gives a fascinating picture of daily life. The architecture had been destroyed by fire in the 10th century, meaning that house plans were preserved, baked hard like ceramic, with objects still inside them. The majority of artefacts found were locally-produced, with large quantities of ceramics of a type known as Early Tana Tradition, which is shared with all East African coastal settlements, as well as sites far into the African hinterland.[8]

The remains of fish bones at Tumbe show the importance of marine resources in the diet, particularly those fish from nearby coral reefs. Burned plant remains show that people were mainly eating local crops, with pearl millet the most important cereal. This contrasts with later centuries, when contacts with the Indian Ocean world began to transform diets: fish came from deeper ocean waters accompanied by rice brought from Asia. During the 8th and 9th centuries, though, sites like Tumbe show that overseas trade was incorporated into a village society, with only minor lifestyle changes.[9]

Yet these small villages inhabited by fishermen and farmers were involved in Indian Ocean trade from the start. The most visible evidence of this is the range of ceramics, coming mainly from the Persian Gulf. Turquoise alkaline glazed wares, made in what is now southern Iraq, are found at sites across the Indian Ocean from the 7th–9th centuries. In East Africa, sherds of these wares are the most common imports; they probably contained date products or oil from the Persian Gulf.[10]

We do not know how trade was structured in East African society at this time. Al-Mas'udi mentions kings or lords in several towns, as well as both Muslim and pagan communities.

28. Bead grinders for shell bead production made of sherds of amphorae from the Middle East. Unguja Ukuu, Zanzibar, ca 700–950 CE (Photo: Jason Hawkes).

29. Beads made from seashells were used in trade with overseas merchants and the African hinterland. Unguja Ukuu, Zanzibar, ca 700–950 CE (Photo: Jason Hawkes).

Turquoise alkaline glazed wares are found in amongst the local ceramics and food remains in villages such as Shanga, Tumbe and Unguja Ukuu, in present-day Tanzania.[11] Thus during this early period of trade it seems that access to foreign goods was available to people across the settlement, without any obvious concentration in the hands of rulers or merchant groups.

Sites in the 8th–9th centuries also produced objects for trade, and production was spread through the settlements. We assume that most of the objects made on the coast were probably being traded into the interior in exchange for the ivory, wood, slaves, and minerals that were moving into the Indian Ocean markets. Most of the objects are difficult to trace archaeologically, like the iron that we know was smelted inside the villages.[12] In addition, shell bead production seems to have been a huge industry, with thousands of bead grinders – ceramic sherds used for grinding down cylinders of shell to be cut into beads – found in all sites of this period, though often the numbers of shell beads are quite low. It seems that the beads were traded onwards, and they are found in the interior, where they would have been exotic luxuries in their own right.[13]

The African villages of the early Swahili coast were true emporia. They were quite humble sites, with a population living on local crops and using local technologies. Although we have some evidence from the medieval histories and geographies for hierarchy and control, archaeology paints a picture of a society in which the profits of trade were available to all. In later centuries, the Swahili would be profoundly influenced by this contact, with the emporia of the coast becoming ever more cosmopolitan. Coral-built architecture, mosques, and the development of a trading elite would all develop in succeeding years, and the coastal population would begin to eat rice, and to style themselves as 'Shirazi', or Persian (derived from the name of the city of Shiraz, in modern Iran), in ancestry.[14] This early period between the 7th and 10th centuries is often ignored in favour of the grander later towns, such as Mombasa and Kilwa, but is a much more particular phenomenon, with foreign luxury trade connecting a village society to a wider world of interaction.

JEREMY GREEN & ATHENA TRAKADAS

Ships of the Indian Ocean

Since antiquity, a wide variety of boats and ships sailed and traded along the coasts of the expansive Indian Ocean world. The trade in foodstuffs, spices, pottery, glass and raw materials like wood, incense and metals increased during the first several centuries BCE/CE.[1] The routes expanded by the early medieval period – forming what has sometimes been called a "Maritime Silk Road" that included the Indian Ocean, Persian Gulf and Red Sea and extended to the China seas.[2] It was this trade that drew Abhara from his home port of Siraf in the Persian Gulf into the dangerous but extremely profitable trade to and from China in the 9th century. Diverse groups participated, with Arab, Indian, Southeast Asian and Chinese vessels all involved.[3] The sources on indigenous Indian Ocean vessels – an archaeological find of a shipwreck, contemporary illustrations, and written records – are from different cultures and technological traditions. In addition to being limited in number, they can be difficult to interpret.

Unlike the Baltic and Mediterranean, the Indian Ocean lacks archaeological finds of shipwrecks – there are hardly any sites dating before the entrance of European ships in the late 15th century.[4] A recent find in Indonesia, however, sheds some light on 9th-century vessels of the region: the Belitung shipwreck, carrying, amongst other things, a cargo of Tang Dynasty ceramic wares.[5] Although its hull is fragmentary, the wood species and "sewn construction" technique indicate an Indian Ocean origin, and its cargo illustrates the voyages between the Persian Gulf and China we know from contemporary texts and trade goods found on land.[6] Arabic texts provide some information on ships' construction: in addition to Buzurg Ibn Shahriyar's book, *The Marvels of the Wonders of India*, *Arabian Nights* includes sea stories, such as the "Seven Voyages of Sindbad the Sailor".[7] Even though these and other stories have their origins in the oral traditions of the early medieval period, their texts also include later additions, making it possible that the details regarding ships might extend over a span of time. It should not be forgotten, either, that these belong to the 'marvels and wonders' genre and information may be 'modified'.[8]

Geographers of the Islamic world, such as al-Ya'qubi (d. 891 CE) and al-Ma'sudi (d. 956 CE) reveal more information. For example, although the planks in ships' hulls in some regions could be nailed together, they tell us that Persian Gulf, Red Sea and Indian Ocean hulls largely had their plank edges sewn together by coir – a detail also mentioned in the Koran.[9] This is confirmed by other sources, for example, the 6th-century Byzantine historian Procopius and the Italian Franciscan missionary, John of Montecorvino (d. 1328).[10]

Few traces of sewn vessels survive today, although the East African *metepe* and the Omani *batil qārib* are examples.[11] This construction builds up a hull of planks that are joined edge-to-edge. Between these edges, bunches of wadding, and perhaps battens, are held in place by sewing them fast with coir

30. Planks of vessels in the Indian Ocean were usually sewn together using coir. Reconstruction of the Belitung wreck, *Jewel of Muscat*, built in Oman in 2009–2010 (Photo: Alessandro Ghidoni).

31. A sailing ship of the Indian Ocean as depicted by Yahya ibn Mahmud al-Wasti in a 1237 CE manuscript of the *Maqāmāt* by al-Hariri of Basra (Bibliothèque nationale de France, manuscript Arabe 5847, folio 119, verso, 1237 / De Agostini Picture Library / The Bridgeman Art Library).

Venetian traveller Marco Polo (d. 1323) notes that ships built at the mouth of the Persian Gulf in Hormuz used wooden dowels to hold the plank edges of sewn boats in place.[15] Today, however, nail joinery is the dominate construction used in wooden vessels in the region.

A copy of the Arabic manuscript called *Maqāmāt* by al-Hariri of Basra, dating to 1237, shows a very detailed illustration of what is generally assumed to be a sewn boat: the horizontal plank edges are periodically marked by pairs of short vertical lines, much like what can be seen on the exteriors of historical and modern sewn boats.[16] In the *Maqāmāt* the vessel appears to have rather straight stem- and sternposts (sometimes called "double-ended" – without a transom), and this general hull shape appears preserved in the modern *būm* vessel type of Kuwait and the *batīl* type in Oman.[17] The medieval Arabic word *khaytiyya* refers to a sewn vessel, and it appears in texts describing vessels of different size in the Red Sea, Persian Gulf, and well as those that sailed to China.[18] Cargo ships are referred to in medieval texts generally as *safīna*, *markab*, and *qārib*, to name a few, and in some cases these terms have been later adopted in different regions to refer to a local type.[19]

What is of great interest is the *Maqāmāt* ship's steering mechanism that consists of an axial rudder on the stern and what appears to be a quarter rudder on the side of the ship. Another copy of the *Maqāmāt*, from Baghdad and dating to ca 1225-1235, shows a

stitching. The stitching is passed through holes pierced all the way through the plank, along its long edges. Frames are then inserted and held fast by stitching; through-beams fore and aft are added across the uppermost planks of the hull.[12]

Many medieval writers theorised as to why vessels in the Indian Ocean were sewn – ranging from the presumed presence of magnetic rocks on the seabed that would make iron nails loosen in a ship's hull to the relative inexpensiveness of coir. Perhaps one of the most convincing arguments is that sewn joinery makes a ship slightly more flexible, and therefore able to endure the weather and seas of its sailing routes.[13] Southeast Asian traditions that entered the Indian Ocean at some unknown point in time joined planks along their edges with dowels and Chinese and perhaps European vessels introduced the use of iron nails.[14] The similar sewn straight stem- and stern-post vessel, although this time without an indication of a quarter rudder.[20] Instead, the axial rudder has lugs attached to the rudder to which ropes are connected and are in turn pulled by the steersman. This system is also seen on some vessels in the Indian Ocean and Persian Gulf in historical times.

Both the *Maqāmāt* illustrations depict grapnel anchors off their bows (an anchor with four or more tines); as the story of Abhara tell us, numbers of these were usually carried on board ships in case one was snagged and lost on the seabed or the crew would have to cut the line in case of emergency. The specific grapnel anchor shape depicted in the manuscripts is also known through archaeological finds of so-called "Indo-Arabian type" anchors. These had long rectangular stone shanks, with holes at each end – the wooden tines passed through one hole and the cable that would attach to a ship's bow passed through the other hole. Many of the stone parts of these anchors are found off the west coast of India, the Arabian Peninsula and in the Persian Gulf, at sites such as Siraf.[21]

We know from texts and iconography that Indian Ocean ships adopted sails quite early, and square sails appear to be the main sail type. Bas-reliefs dating to the 9th century on the Buddhist temple at Borobudur in central Java show what appear to be vessels with two masts and square sails.[22] Ibn Jubayr,

32. Almost all modern wooden sailing vessels in the Indian Ocean and Persian Gulf are now constructed using nail joinery, like these two abandoned *jalbut*s in a shipyard in Muharraq, Bahrain (Photo: Athena Trakadas).

a geographer writing in the later 12th century, records the use of square sails on the Red Sea.[23]

The 1237 copy of al-Hariri's *Maqāmāt* shows the vessel's sail being controlled by a steersman who holds onto lines, but its shape is very difficult to interpret. In the Baghdad *Maqāmāt*, the ship appears to have a broken mast; however, on closer inspection the upper part of the mast could be stepped, with a possible scarf joint that would have attached it to the lower part. The sail is attached at the top of the mast, and could represent matting – woven coconut, bamboo, flax or palm leaves – still used for sails on vessels in the Indian Ocean. Wool sails were used in Mesopotamia, and although cotton is known, it is not mentioned in relation to sails in any contemporary manuscripts.[24]

No medieval Arabic source mentions the lateen or triangular sail in the Indian Ocean.[25] The definite appearance of this sail type occurs later, when vessels from the Indian sub-continent merged with the Arab tradition; it is commonly associated with the modern *dhow* ship-type. There was also a settee, a lateen-like sail with the leading part cut off so that it is quadrilateral in shape and thus something between the square sail and the lateen.[26] It is possible that these three sail types were used simultaneously for a time, and certainly this appears to be the case after the arrival of European ships into the Indian Ocean in the late 15th century. However, it is the lack of information prior to the arrival of Europeans into the Indian Ocean that makes this, and so many other technological details regarding ship construction and types in this sea, difficult questions to answer.

TOM VOSMER

The Belitung shipwreck and *Jewel of Muscat*

It is a common misconception, generated by reports from medieval European travellers as well as a Euro-centric view of the superiority of western nautical technology that the sewn craft of the Indian Ocean were, as Marco Polo remarked, "wretched affairs".[1] The vessels that Abhara likely sailed seven times from Siraf to China were in fact, sewn boats. Only one example has yet been found in the archaeological record: the Belitung shipwreck from the 9th century, discovered in 1998 in Indonesian waters. The timber species, stitching cordage and construction technique (edge-sewn planks, lashed frames) of the wreck's hull mark it as having been built in the western Indian Ocean. It contained an amazingly rich cargo of Chinese ceramics, spices,

33. *Jewel of Muscat*, a reconstruction of a 9th-century sewn ship from the western Indian Ocean, on her voyage from Oman to Singapore (Photo: Robert Jackson).

34. Inside (top): the lashed framing of *Jewel of Muscat*. Outside (bottom): the edge-sewn planks (Photos: Alessandro Ghidoni).

some Islamic ceramics, bronze mirrors, and the most significant hoard of gold and silver objects to be recovered from a single site outside China.[2]

While perhaps prone to some leaking, sewn ships were marvels of subtle engineering: strong, resilient, and capable of sailing courses denied to European vessels of the same period. With sewn ships, Indian Ocean merchant sailors were able to establish by the 8th century the longest sea-trading route in the world, from the Middle East to China.[3] The sailing from Oman to Singapore of *Jewel of Muscat*, a ship reconstruction based on the remains of the ship-find from Belitung, illustrates the seaworthiness and weatherliness of such craft.

In the design and construction of *Jewel*, in Oman in 2009–2010, strict attention was paid to the Belitung archaeological evidence – species of timbers, stitching hole size and spacing, stitching pattern, size and spacing of beams, thickness of planking, spacing of frames. But some information, such as the configuration of the stern and the design of the rig, was missing.

ABHARA'S WORLD   59

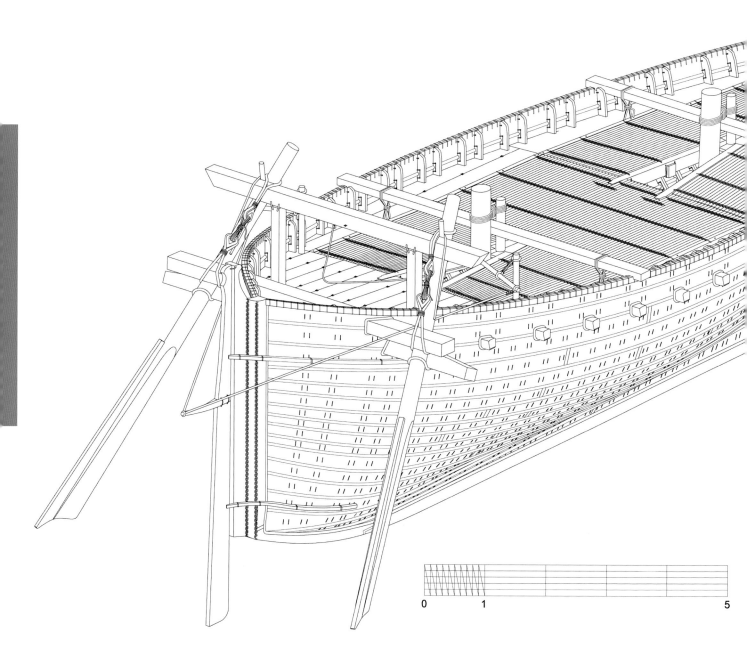

35. View of the hull of *Jewel of Muscat*, showing the deck plan, and twin quarter rudders and axial rudder (design by Nick Burningham, Tom Vosmer and Mike Flecker).

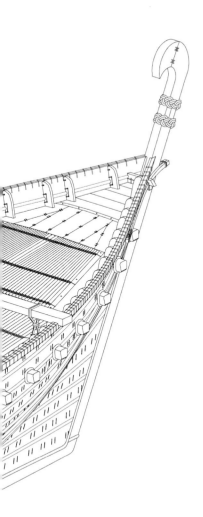

To fill in blanks, clues were derived from medieval texts, iconography, ethnographic sources and naval architecture principles. The reconstruction was 18.5 m long, 6.5 m beam with a displacement of 55 tons.

It is another common misconception that Indian Ocean ships had always had settee sails (a quadrilateral lateen sail). In fact, there is no irrefutable evidence for settee sails in the western Indian Ocean until at least 1500.[4] Sixteenth-century iconography consistently shows Arab, Persian and Indian ships with square sails. Islamic ships illustrated in the Lopo Homem's *Atlas* of 1519 all have square sails.[5] Contemporary and even later ship graffiti show only square sails, much like those used in Nordic boats.[6]

Thus, *Jewel* was square-rigged on two masts, using cotton canvas sails. This rig provided flexibility in setting the sails and tuning. The double-ended hull form of *Jewel*, fine at both ends and deep-V in section, enabled the ship to resist leeway and sail up to 51° into the wind.

The era when the Belitung ship and Abhara sailed saw a technological development in the Indian Ocean, a transition from quarter rudders (mounted on the side of the hull) to an axial rudder fitted on the stern. Roughly contemporary illustrations, such the *Maqāmāt* by al-Hariri from 1273, show both systems in use on single vessels. In Europe, a similar transition took place a couple of hundred years later.[7] Taking a cue from this, *Jewel* had twin quarter rudders and an axial rudder, offering the opportunity to experiment with both systems.

Sailing the ship provided occasion for experimentation with life on board and traditional navigation in the 9th century. On the first leg of the passage, goats and chickens provided fresh food. It was found that the chickens were more trouble than they were worth – too little protein for the care required. The goats, though providing a ready source of meat, had to be carefully monitored as they displayed a fondness to devour parts of the sewn ship.

Although built as a 9th-century ship, *Jewel* boasted an array of modern instruments to monitor performance and offer a measure of safety through modern communications and GPS navigation. But practice with the *kamal*, a medieval Arab instrument to measure latitude, provided perspective on the efficacy of the instrument as well as the skill required to navigate.

Data feeds from instruments measuring wind speed, boat speed, heading, current, angle of heel, speed made good and windward ability logged the performance of the vessel. Overall, the vessel handled better and was faster than anticipated. She weathered the heavy seas and winds of cyclone Laila, though taking on up to 6 tons of water a day. Arriving safely from Muscat to Singapore after a 7,000 km passage, *Jewel* proved the remarkable abilities of medieval sewn-plank vessels, such as Abhara himself might have captained.

JULIAN WHITEWRIGHT

Maritime rhythms of the monsoon

The Indian Ocean maritime world of Abhara moved to a unique rhythm based upon the prevailing seasonal weather patterns. These are known individually as a monsoon, derived from the Arabic *mawsim*, meaning a fixed time of year.[1] Two main monsoons can be identified: blowing from the north-east in the winter and the south-west during the summer with a variable weather season in between.[2]

The two monsoons are very different from each other. The north-easterly monsoon of the winter is characterised by dry, steady, relatively gentle winds which encourage sailing throughout its duration. Meanwhile, the south-westerly summer monsoon is wet, violent and characterised by storms and strong wind with sailing only feasible at the beginning and end, in the late spring and early autumn. Unlike in the Mediterranean and Northern Europe, then, sailing in the Indian Ocean tended to avoid the summer months of June, July and August. The switch in overall wind direction resulting from the monsoon patterns means that it is possible to sail on the Indian Ocean with a constantly favourable wind, if done in conjunction with the monsoon rhythms. Using favourable winds as much as possible was important because medieval Indian Ocean sailing vessels could only sail to windward in lighter winds but were efficient when sailing with the wind, being able to average as much as 11 kph on extended voyages and with an even higher top speed in very good conditions.[3]

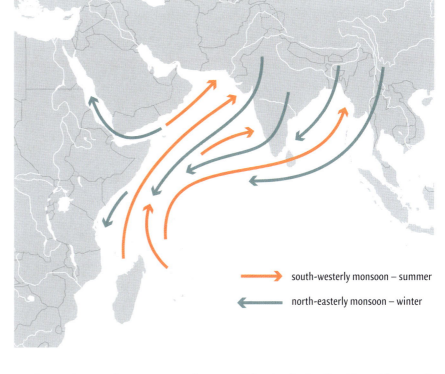

36. Ships in the Indian Ocean, like this modern lateen rigged vessel off Zanzibar, Tanzania, have used the seasonality of the monsoon winds for millennia (Photo: Søren M. Sindbæk).

Map 5. The monsoon systems of the Indian Ocean.

south-westerly monsoon – summer
north-easterly monsoon – winter

The monsoon is mentioned in the *Periplus Maris Erythraei*, a Greek text written in the mid 1st century CE by someone with intimate knowledge of the Red Sea, Persian Gulf, Bay of Bengal and Arabian Sea.[4] However, our best information for using the monsoon comes from Ibn Majid, a master navigator from what is now the United Arab Emirates, writing in the 15th century.[5] Ibn Majid describes the routes around the Indian Ocean and lists the times of the year when vessels should depart certain ports in order to arrive safely at their destination. From his work, we can construct a seasonal timetable whereby ships departed from ports in the Gulf like Siraf and southwestern India during the autumn, sailing to East African ports like Zanzibar on the north-easterly monsoon and returning during the spring on the first winds of the south-westerly monsoon. Vessels from Red Sea ports like Aylah would sail south in late summer, using the tail-end of the south-westerly monsoon to sail to southwestern Indian ports, returning again in December and January when they would have the favourable winds of the north-easterly monsoon. The voyage between the Red Sea and East Africa could be made using a combination of the two monsoons and a stopover at a port such as Aden in Yemen.

Voyages eastward, to Southeast Asia and China, probably via the Straits of Melaka, also fitted within this timetable. Vessels could leave southern India in late December, arriving in the China Sea in April or May with an arrival in Guangzhou for the summer. The return voyage would depart in the autumn and cross the Bay of Bengal in January. A vessel sailing from a Gulf port might take a year and a half in good weather to complete the round trip to China and back. In all the examples voyages could be made directly, or by stopping to trade at ports. In this way the two monsoons provided the mariners of the Indian Ocean with a means to sail around with a degree of relative certainty and predictability, arriving in specific ports at specific times, which perhaps contrasts to the seafaring of more northern seas.

JASON HAWKES &
STEPHANIE WYNNE-JONES

India in Africa

In countries all around the Indian Ocean 'foreign' objects provide us with evidence for links between these different parts of the world in the past. We often think of these objects as commodities of trade, but they speak equally of customs, ideas and values that were exchanged by cultures and societies.

Red Polished Ware is a type of extremely fine quality Indian pottery that has been found at a number of sites in East Africa dating to the 7th to 9th centuries.[1] The number of Red Polished Ware vessels in Africa is very small, indicating that they may not have been main objects of trade, but were brought by merchants for their own personal use. Interestingly, pottery that is very similar in both fabric and shapes to Indian Red Polished Ware was also produced locally in ports and settlements along the East African coast,[2] but not further inland, which suggests that they were used by people and communities connected with the Indian Ocean. There are bowls, cups and dishes that would have been used by individuals for eating and drinking. So instead of just trade in ceramics, these objects point to much broader types of interaction.

Carnelian beads are one of a vast array of beads that were traded across the Indian Ocean.[3] Their source is often very difficult to identify, yet most appear to have been manufactured in northwestern India, probably in Gujarat.[4] This is home to the richest source of carnelian and an unchanged tradition of making beads that can be traced back at least four thousand years. These beads are found at sites in East Africa from at least the 7th century onwards, perhaps even earlier. Carnelian beads are found only in high-status contexts, mainly in coastal towns linked to merchant elites, or in rich burials in the hinterland. They are also a part of a much larger corpus of glass beads, many of which came from India.[5] These 'trade-wind' beads were a key commodity of the pre-modern period. The beads travelled easily, and around 1000, made it as far inland as Lake Victoria. Similar beads are also found at many Indian sites,[6] suggesting that with all of this trade and interaction across the Indian Ocean, people developed shared tastes and aesthetics as well as shared understandings of value which could have meant that beads functioned almost as a currency.

37. Indian beads from Unguja Ukuu, Zanzibar, Tanzania. Carnelian, ca 700–950 CE (Photo: Ian Cartwright, School of Archaeology, University of Oxford).

HELLE HORSNÆS

Changing hands: the Skovsholm *dirham* hoard

38. Hoard of 151 *dirhams* from Skovsholm, Bornholm, Denmark. Silver. Deposited after 855 CE (National Museum of Denmark, The Royal Collection of Coins and Medals).

Silver *dirham* coins are a tangible link between the 9th-century worlds of Ohthere and Abhara. Throughout the Indian Ocean, Mediterranean and in Northern Europe, merchants and sailors were familiar with *dirhams* brought from the Islamic caliphates that extended from present-day Spain to Afghanistan. They were carried north to the Baltic by Scandinavian and local traders, dealing in commodities including slaves and furs, who had followed the great rivers of Eastern Europe from the Caspian and Black Seas. Many hoards have been found in particular on the Swedish Baltic island of Gotland, including the largest known Viking-Age hoard, consisting of more than 14,000 *dirhams*, along with silver jewellery and scrap bronze.[1] Altogether, some 300,000 Arabic silver coins are recorded in hoards or single finds in Northern Europe.[2]

During the 9th century *dirhams* from the large mints in Madinat as-Salam (Baghdad) and al-Muhammadiyya (near Tehran) are abundant in the North, and in the first third of the century coins from mints in North Africa are also common. Older coins struck by rulers of the Umayyad Caliphate during the mid 7th to mid 8th centuries, and even older ones of the Sasanian Empire (centred in present-day Iran), ending in the mid 7th century, were all struck of good silver and still circulated alongside coins of the Abbasid Caliphate (750–1258 CE). Occasionally there are imitative *dirhams* struck in the Khazar Empire, in the steppes north of the Caucasus.[3]

The Skovsholm hoard, found on the Danish Baltic island of Bornholm in 2012, is the largest *dirham* hoard from the 9th century found in Denmark. It contained 151 coins deposited in the ground after 855.[4] The hoard was located next to a natural spring, and excavations have revealed substantial building remains close by. Most of the hoard's coins had been cut or broken into fragments of 'hack silver', as they were exchanged in the northern lands according to weight rather than to their nominal value. The Skovsholm hoard contains a wide range of *dirhams*: the oldest coin was struck by the Sasanian king Khusrau II (r. 591–628), while the latest coins were struck by the Abbasid caliph Al-Mutawakkil in 240 AH (854/855). The Sasanian coins bear an image of the ruler, in profile, during whose reign they were minted, with inscriptions in Middle Persian, or Pahlavi, script.[5] The coins from the Islamic caliphates, however, are without pictures. They carry quotes from the Koran in Arabic Kufic script, as well as information about who was caliph at the time, and when and where they were minted. The mints ranged from present-day Uzbekistan to Morocco, and their coins linked people to an even wider world.

THEODOSIOS' WORLD

"Then the emperor Theophilos, not accepting defeat … despatched to the king of Francia the *patrikios* Theodosios, also known as Baboutzikos, asking for brave and well-stocked armies from there …"

Theophanes Continuatus, *Chronographia*, 11th century

JONATHAN SHEPARD

Theodosios' voyages

The senior civil servants of 9th-century Constantinople – capital of the Eastern Roman or Byzantine Empire until 1453 – were in much the same position as their modern counterparts: they conducted administration, examined tax-rolls, and counselled the Byzantine emperor. But on the empire's borders lived fearsome 'barbarians'. Recognising their inability to micromanage from afar, emperors were apt to send 'trouble-shooters' capable of improvising treaties and alliances with neighbouring polities or potentates. One such 'trouble-shooter' during the reign of Theophilos (829–842 CE) was Theodosios Baboutzikos, a relation of the emperor's wife who held the lofty court-title *patrikios*.[1] In 840, Theodosios embarked on a long and dangerous voyage. His mission: to recruit allies from Venice and further north against an outburst of sea-borne Muslim piracy and raiding.

Glimpses of Theodosios come from three seals – probably attached to letters he wrote – found in Northern Europe. They name the issuer as the *patrikios* Theodosios, and his office as *Chartoularios tou Bestiariou* – meaning roughly 'Chief Secretary to the (Imperial) Stores and Treasury'. Byzantine and western chronicles add some details of his journeys, while the seals show how far north of the Mediterranean world his interests reached, to the Baltic Sea and beyond, regions virtually unfathomed by Byzantine statesmen only a few decades before.

The western half of the Roman Empire had come under the dominion of ambitious Germanic warlords in

39. One of the important monuments of the Byzantine Empire was Hagia Sophia (Holy Wisdom). From 537 until 1453, this church was at the heart of the walled city of Constantinople and a short distance away from *Portus Theodosiacus*, where Theodosios likely set sail for Venice; it was later converted into a mosque and then a museum (Photo: Athena Trakadas).

the 5th and 6th centuries. Christian Byzantium's provinces, from Egypt to Cilicia (in modern southeast Turkey), were overrun in the 7th century by Muslims united in their new faith. The Umayyad and subsequent Abbasid Caliphates' territorial expansion pressed into Central Asia, until the battle of Talas in 751; and also towards the Volga steppes, where the semi-nomadic Khazars defeated them in the same era. It extended across North Africa, crossing the Strait of Gibraltar in 711. Byzantium, with its capital in Constantinople on the Bosporus joining the Mediterranean and Black Seas, now stood alone, in a 'state of emergency'.[2] Yet it maintained, besides internal order and regular tax-collection, a series of enclaves and islands reaching from the southern Balkans across the central Mediterranean to the Balearic Islands.

Despite Muslim raiding in the eastern Mediterranean, cross-border exchanges never abated altogether and, by the earlier 9th century, maritime commerce was picking up. A Byzantine chronicle has it that Emperor Theophilos saw a huge merchantman anchored in a Constantinople harbour – a ship which probably came from some Muslim-ruled port. Theophilos, learning the ship was his wife's and exclaiming, "Who ever saw an emperor of the Romans [Byzantines] or his wife engaging in trade?", had ship and cargo burnt![3] The tale contains a grain of truth: privileged Byzantines were dabbling in trade, as recent excavations in one of Constantinople's harbours, modern Yenikapı in Istanbul, have shown.[4] From Constantinople and provincial ports, goods were shipped to the eastern and western Mediterranean, and also across the Black Sea. Leading inhabitants of towns like Ragusa on the Dalmatian coast were enthusiastic visitors to the imperial court in the 9th century. From around 800, goods from ports around the Mediterranean began arriving in sizable quantities at Venice's lagoon and surrounding areas, as recent excavations have shown.[5] Venice was also near well-travelled routes leading through the Alps to the Middle Danube and, ultimately, the Baltic.

The downside of the boom was that the waterways attracted predators. A band of adventurers from Umayyad Spain seized Alexandria but eventually surrendered to the authorities of the Abbasid Caliphate, who let them depart provided that they left other Muslim-controlled lands alone. Descending on Crete in 827, they took over a fortress and then other parts of the island, rebuffing Theophilos' counter-attacks.[6] Crete became a pirate base. Further west, the emirs of Kairouan in modern Tunisia had their eyes on Byzantine Sicily. They launched an invasion and, by 829, were established on the west coast and inland. Palermo soon fell, and fleets from Tunisia infested the heel of Italy. In 841 one emir made Bari his stronghold, little more than 24 hours' sail from the Dalmatian coast.

Theophilos was hard-put to defend his empire's western approaches. A huge army led by Caliph al-Mu'tasim sacked the key city of Amorium, in modern central-western Turkey, in 838. Besides humiliating the emperor, Amorium's fall raised the question of what could prevent resumption of the Abbasid army's drive northwards into the Volga and Don Steppes. The Khazars posed the principal barrier. From tolls on traffic across their lands they had grown rich, and their military capability was formidable. Among the traders passing through were Scandinavians who had migrated east from the Baltic, to regions still bearing their name: 'Russia' is called after these people, known to Finnish-speakers in the northern-most forests as *Ruotsi*, and to Slavs further south as *Rus*. The Byzantines soon became aware of them through their activities in Khazaria, with which the empire had close, if uneasy, relations. In fact, individual Scandinavians made careers down south: two persons bearing the Nordic-derived name 'Ingeros' are attested in early 9th-century Byzantium. It is even possible that a *Rus* war-band negotiated the riverways to and raided in the Black Sea in the 830s.[7]

Facing all these risks, Theophilos launched several initiatives in the later 830s. He sent an embassy to the Umayyad ruler at Cordoba, proposing collaboration.[8] And he sent a mission to build a fortress for the Khazars on the Lower Don: Byzantine technical expertise could help regulate steppe-nomads at river crossings, while serving notice to the Abbasid Caliphate of imperial concern with the region.

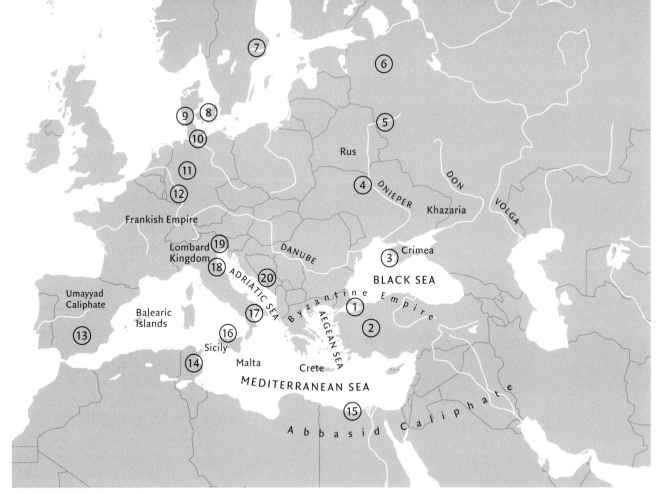

Map 6. Theodosios' world: 1 Constantinople, 2 Amorium, 3 Cherson, 4 Kiev, 5 Gnezdovo, 6 Riurikovoe Gorodischche, 7 Birka, 8 Tissø, 9 Ribe, 10 Hedeby, 11 Ingelheim, 12 Trier, 13 Cordoba, 14 Kairouan, 15 Alexandria, 16 Palermo, 17 Taranto, 18 Comacchio, 19 Venice, 20 Ragusa

In 838, Theophilos received an embassy from the ruler of the Rus, then based far to the north, probably at Riurikovoe Gorodischche (near modern Novgorod). How the envoys reached Constantinople is uncertain – perhaps following trade-routes along the Don to the Black Sea coast, perhaps over the steppes to the Byzantine outpost of Cherson. What we know is that Theophilos included them in an embassy sent to the western emperor, Louis the Pious, at his court at Ingelheim.

"[The] embassy's business was to confirm a treaty of peace and perpetual friendship and fellowship between the two emperors and their subjects; ... He (Theophilos) also sent with them (the legates) certain men who said that they, that is, their people were called "Rhos"; their king, known as the chaganus, had despatched them to him (Theophilos) for the sake of friendship, so they claimed. He requested through the fore-mentioned letter that with the emperor's favour they might receive every facility and assistance in travelling through his empire, seeing that on the routes by which they had reached him in Constantinople they had been among barbarous and most savage peoples of exceedingly great ferocity, and he was unwilling that they should return by them, lest they should come to grief. The emperor, investigating more diligently the reason for their arrival, discovered that they belonged to the people of the Swedes (Sueonum). Reckoning that they were spies of that realm and of ours rather than seekers after friendship, he decided that they should be kept under detention, until such time as it could be truly established whether they had come in good faith or not." – Annales Bertiniani [9]

A small group of silver and copper coins of Theophilos unearthed at Hedeby, Birka, Styrnäs (Ångermanland) and Riurikovoe Gorodischche could mark the approximate 'footprints' of the Rus envoys returning to their ruler; low-value Byzantine coins like these are extremely rare in Scandinavia, and could be small change, lost or discarded en route. [10]

Not long after despatching the embassy escorting the Rus to Louis, Theophilos sent Theodosios Baboutzikos to Venice.

"Then in the month of May at the sixth hour the sun was obscured and an eclipse occurred [5 May, 840]. Furthermore at this time Theodosios the patrikios, coming to Venice from Constantinople, invested the Doge Peter with the insignia of the dignity of spatharius. He spent a whole year there, on the emperor's behalf entreating the Doge not to refuse to concede him an expeditionary force for overcoming the Saracens [Muslims]. This the Doge did not demur from doing willingly. Then in all haste he strove to make ready sixty ships of war, and sent them all the way to Taranto, where Saba, the leader of the Saracens, was lurking with a very great army. However, nearly all the Venetians were captured and killed by the host of Saracens." – John the Deacon, Cronaca Veneziana [11]

"In those days Theodosios the patrikios came to Venice and, in the name of the emperor, made the Doge Peter a spatharius of the empire; and he asked the Venetians swiftly to see to preparations for making war against the Saracens." – Andreas Dandolo, Chronica per extensum descripta [12]

Theodosios Baboutzikos does not seem to have had previous experience of representing the emperor. But, as these passages show, he enjoyed Theophilos' trust and he was charged with inducing the Doge, Pietro Tradonico, to mount an expedition against the 'Saracens'. Unfortunately, the Venetians suffered crushing defeat at the Muslims' hands, many perishing.[13] Theodosios spent "a whole year" in Venice, probably from the early spring of 840. Although persuading Pietro to marshal a fleet may have taken time, this would scarcely have required 12 months. His lengthy stay implies activities more elaborate than doling out money, although the Constantinopolitan mint was one responsibility of the Chartoularios tou Bestiariou. Other duties included assembling, storing and allocating military and especially naval equipment.[14] So Theodosios could well have contributed to the construction or refitting of the "ships of war" sent to Taranto. It may be no accident that in the era of Doge Pietro two "warships … called in the Greek language zalandriae" (i.e., chelandia) were built, "the

40. The present interior of Hagia Sophia reflects it history as a place of worship for two religions. Mosaics of angels, the Virgin, Christ and emperors now share space with medallions of sultans and a mihrab. Rich marble, brought by ship from the nearby island of Proconnesos, was used throughout the building's construction (Photo: Athena Trakadas).

like of which was never before seen in Venice".[15] We cannot be sure they were built under Theodosios' supervision, but this seems probable.

It is likely that Theodosios returned to Constantinople to confer with the emperor and be briefed for his next mission: an embassy to the western emperor, now Lothar, to propose marriage between his son Louis and one of Theophilos' daughters. This was uncommonly generous: Byzantine emperors seldom conceded a princess "born in the Purple Chamber" to foreign dynasties. From Theophilos' perspective, the concession was worthwhile, if Lothar acceded to his envoy's proposal: a massive Frankish expedi-

THEODOSIOS' WORLD 71

41. The Basilica of Constantine in the city of Trier, Germany, where Theodosios had an audience with Lothar on his mission to the Frankish Kingdom in 842 CE (Photo: Werner Berthold).

tion to fight the Saracen armies.[16] An obvious target was North Africa, the base for most of the Saracens then overrunning Sicily. And a joint-expedition against "the common enemies" is proposed in a papyrus preserved at Paris' monastery of St. Denis. This letter from a Byzantine emperor to a western ruler concerns an expedition that would involve the latter's son and strike against the Saracens, renewing God's glory.[17] No names survive on what remains of the papyrus, but its contents match the chronicles' accounts of Theodosios' mission.[18] So it is probable that Theodosios delivered the papyrus to Louis' father, Lothar, upon being received at his court in Trier, between 16 June and 29 August, 842.[19] By the time he did so, the emperor was dead, and Theodosios himself expired after he had negotiated the betrothal of Louis to Theophilos' daughter. The embassy's significance is clear from the very fact that Byzantine chronicles mention Theodosios Baboutzikos and his objective of operations against the Muslims: few embassies receive such detailed attention.

"Then the emperor Theophilos, not accepting defeat and disgrace at the hands of the Agarenes [Muslims], despatched to the king of Francia [Lothar] the *patrikios* Theodosios, also known as Baboutzikos, asking for brave and well-stocked armies from there.... Now if he had had proof of the strength and power of the nations upon whom he called – and the king had gladly accepted the idea of an allied force for the emperor – then once again Theophilos the luckless (a nickname acquired from being ever the loser in war) would have campaigned against the Agarenes. However, his envoy Theodosios' departure from this life occurred before this could happen. Theodosios' demise did not make for the passage of that army to the reigning city [Constantinople], and the triumph of dysentery over the emperor made him mortally ill, and not for his advance to arms." – Theophanes Continuatus, *Chronographia*[20]

"Theophilos... could not sit idly by and, unable to take the fall of Amorium with equanimity, he sought the time and the means to wreak vengeance on his foe. Accordingly, he sent to the king of Francia the *patrikios* Theodosios, from the family of the Baboutzikoi, asking for an allied army to be sent to him and also for the despatch of a significant force to ravage certain parts of Libya belonging to the Commander of the Faithful [the Caliph]. But the embassy was to no effect, for Theodosios' life ended while he was on his journey." – John Skylitzes, *Synopsis Historion*[21]

"Lothar received at Trier legates of the Greeks [led by Theodosios Baboutzikos], and having dismissed them, at the time of this same assembly he moved his residence to the palace known as Thionville." – *Annales Bertiniani*[22]

"To this man (Lothar) the Constantinopolitan emperor Theophilos sent legates, promising to give his daughter as wife for his son Louis. But while these matters were being transacted, Theophilos Augustus died, in the thirteenth year of his reign." – Andreas Dandolo, *Chronica per extensum descripta*[23]

The missions of Theodosios to Venice and the Frankish emperor's court had comparable aims, to prevent the Muslims from overrunning southern Italy as well as Sicily. Emperor Theophilos could ill afford ships or soldiers, but Byzantine diplomacy disposed of gold, know-how and connections. In redirecting the Rus envoys to the west, Theophilos could have had more practical aims than simply demonstrating those connections. He may have been appraising overland routes from Venice to the Baltic, contemplating recruitment of Nordic seamen for warfare against the Muslims; whilst heading for home through Viking regions, the Rus envoys might encourage successive hosts to make contact with him or his agents. Such a scheme was scarcely more far-fetched than the project Theodosios outlined to Lothar. Enlisting Viking naval skills was probably already on Theophilos' agenda, when he sent the Rus envoys home via Francia and the Baltic.

Three seals of Theodosios Baboutzikos have been found at Ribe and Tissø in Denmark and at Hedeby in Germany; they were most probably issued by him while on assignment, sealing letters he sent. One cannot exclude the possibility that all three seals and their documents were sent during Theodosios' embassy to the Frankish court, but he could equally well have issued them from Venice in 840. Indeed, Theodosios could have sent messages to the Nordic world on each visit to the west, seeing that his seals found at Ribe and Tissø came from a different *boulloterion*, or seal stamp, from the one that stamped the third seal.[24]

Precisely whom the sealed messages were meant for is unclear. One – even all – could have been addressed to the predominant Danish king in the earlier 840s. Horic was at peace with Lothar, and perhaps Theodosios, on behalf of Theophilos, dreamed of an alliance between western emperor and Danish king close enough for them to liaise with Byzantine personnel against the Muslims, vessels being prepared for them at Venice. Theodosios was well-qualified: a bureau comparable to his own, the 'Treasury' (*Eidikon*), would provide for the refitting of nine Rus vessels in preparation for an expedition to Crete in 949;[25] around that time, hundreds of Rus participated in an expedition aimed ultimately at Sicily.[26] One cannot, however, be sure that all the messages despatched by Theodosios were intended for King Horic. Tissø may have been an occasional residence of the king, but residence by a noble or minor royal cannot be ruled out.[27] At any rate the other seals, each from a different *boulloterion*, were found at Ribe and Hedeby and were probably despatched at different times. These bustling emporia, although under the king's aegis, were not places where he regularly held court. That the seals were probably sent at different times, and their find-spots in emporia, suggest addressees other than Horic. Theodosios probably cast his net widely, to Danish magnates; commanders of any large fleet frequenting Ribe and Hedeby; or remoter potentates. Hedeby would have been a convenient embarkation-point for voyages to the Swedes or Rus. There has been found at Riurikovoe Gorodishche a Byzantine commander's seal datable to the first half of the 9th century, besides a copper coin of Theophilos.[28] These could have something to do with Theodosios' enterprise.

Quite what Byzantium's emperor and Theodosios Baboutzikos envisaged is hard to determine. They might well have considered enlisting Vikings to crew vessels constructed at Venice, or portaging boats between Frankish riverways to the Mediterranean coast, and circumnavigation of the Iberian Peninsula was conceivable. They had probably heard from their Rus visitors in 839 of the distances Viking seafarers covered, probing into the North Atlantic. Incitement of one group of 'barbarians' against another was stock-in-trade of Byzantine diplomacy. One aim of the embassy arriving at Cordoba in 839/40 was to incite Emir 'Abd ar-Rahman to send his fleet as an ally in the struggle for Sicily.[29] A Viking raid on North Africa would have given Theophilos' enemies something to think about, disrupting their attacks on Sicily. No such scheme materialised, but one unintended consequence of the messaging of Theodosios and his emissaries may have been the Viking raid on Seville of 844. The marauders hailed from the Loire estuary, not the Danish lands, but news circulated fast and far. So it is quite possible that gifts of gold accompanying the seals found at Ribe, Hedeby and Tissø, and word of the riches attainable in southern waters, whetted appetites. The Byzantines did not 'kick-start' Viking adventurism, but perhaps they gave it a push.

SAURO GELICHI

The sea of Venice: new cities and the Adriatic Mediterranean economy

42. An interpretation of how the Adriatic lagoonal settlement of Comacchio would have looked in the 8th century (Universita Ca' Foscari – Venice).

Before Venice The Byzantine *patrikios* Theodosios Baboutzikos arrived in Venice from Constantinople in 840 CE and, according to the written sources, remained there a year.[1]

Venice was a new city that had not existed in classical antiquity. It had surprisingly sprung up in the midst of a lagoon in the upper part of the Adriatic Sea – an unlikely spot for a traditional city, but a characteristic location for a newly developing maritime society. At a time interpreted by modern scholars as a general decline of established Mediterranean towns,[2] the northern Adriatic appears instead to have been experiencing unusual 'ferment'. This phenomenon was not generally connected with the ancient urban centres, but seemed to favour new spaces, once uninhabited (or sparsely populated): often marginal sites, such as lagoons, but in excellent locations for commerce (inland and along the coast) and far enough away from the existing centres of strong political powers. These 'grey zones' favoured the emergence of new communities and new aristocracies, oriented in the construction of new opportunities related to transport and navigation, but they were not yet totally disconnected from land ownership.

Venice was not an isolated incident. To the south 160 km, another lagoonal settlement with very similar characteristics developed slightly earlier: Comacchio. While the archaeology of Venice's earliest times is still elusive, Comacchio is well known archaeologically and can serve for comparison. Recent excavations at Comacchio have shown that a settlement on small islands had suddenly developed between the 6th and 7th centuries. Archaeological finds show that it was economically oriented and crafts were a mainstay. At the beginning of the 8th century, Comacchio was stable enough to deal directly with the Lombard Kingdom in northern Italy for trading on the Po River and its tributaries. This is attested by an exceptional

document, the so-called "Capitulary of *Liutprandus*", a text that indicates the tolls that the ships from Comacchio had to pay the Lombards in a number of river ports. Comacchio's merchants exported mainly salt, which they, like the Venetians, collected from the nearby salt marshes. Excavations have also revealed that high-quality glass and metal items, such as cameos in glass or bronze letters were manufactured, surely for trade. Also traded were spices, oil and *garum* (a fish sauce appreciated in antiquity). Some of these products were carried in ceramic containers, or amphorae, which have been found in large quantities in excavations at the city. These amphorae, which come mainly from the Aegean Sea and perhaps the Black Sea, were traded by Byzantine merchants who had reached Comacchio but not yet the far northern Adriatic.[3]

Comacchio in the 8th century was an economically oriented centre, similar in some respects to Northern European settlements such as Hedeby or Kaupang, emerging in the same period, although in different historical and political contexts.[4] Comacchio seems to tell the earliest stage of what would be the future, and, along with Venice, documents an intriguing phenomenon that has no equal in the Mediterranean at this time.

Venice and similar places in the region had gathered speed a century or so before Theodosios' voyage here from Constantinople. In the beginning of the 9th century, the 'new city' of the lagoon had been in conflict with the Franks, but following a peace in 814 the aristocracies of the lagoon hinged between two worlds: the Byzantine Empire (upon whom they still formally depended) and the Frankish Empire (to whom they paid more attention because of new economic opportunities).

Before Theodosios Venice was born 'officially' in 810-11 when *Agnellus Partecipatius* was appointed Doge and a new

THEODOSIOS' WORLD   75

ducal palace was built.[5] But settlements in the Venice lagoon, like Torcello, had already been developing slowly between the 5th and 8th centuries, according to an interesting process of selection and centralisation, especially in the north. The reasons for this progressive growth were due to three main factors: economy, security and isolation. The lagoon had become important economically for its salt production[6] and for trade, first along the northern Adriatic coast (from Istria to Ravenna) and then into the hinterland through the Po River and its tributaries – the river serving as a corridor between the eastern Mediterranean and Northern and Western Europe. The lagoon itself was a protected and secure place for vessels, even serving as the seat of an important Byzantine fleet during the late 6th to late 8th centuries. Additionally, Venice was located some distance from the existing strong 'centres of power' in the region, and this isolation may have facilitated the growth of its own relatively autonomous identity.[7]

But what did the merchants in the northern Adriatic get in return? Perhaps the farms in the Lombard region were producing enough agricultural goods that their surpluses could be traded down the river. Or perhaps Comacchio and other contemporary small settlements in the Venetian lagoon like Torcello dealt only in long-distance maritime trade:[8] terminals receiving goods from afar, independent of the economy of the agricultural hinterland. However, connections into the hinterland are traceable by the presence of globular amphorae and a 'Comacchio type' ceramic in several cities of the interior (such as Cremona, Verona, Milan) and in some monasteries (as Nonantola).

In spite of a fragmentation of the economic and productive structures that takes place during the 7th century, signs of recovery can be seen in the exploitation of land ownership especially in the Po Valley.[9] A clue may be sought, although still indirect and archaeologically faint, just in the foundation of new monasteries in the late Lombard period. Monasteries were related directly to the king or to the highest aristocracy that from the start might have been active agents in a re-organisation and ownership of the territory.

A new perspective in the Adriatic Mediterranean After the peace between the Frankish and Byzantine Empires in 814, a new scenario appears in the northern Adriatic. In this area, certainly among the most dynamic in the Mediterranean, Venice emerges as a powerful lagoonal city, eventually in the 13th and 14th centuries controlling its own maritime empire spanning several seas. But does the situation in the northern Adriatic reflect the general situation of the Mediterranean, or at least that part of the Mediterranean still under Byzantine control, when Theodosios arrived from Constantinople in the 9th century? It does not seem so.

The situation in the southern Adriatic might have been different, but there are few sites here that have been archaeologically investigated. Butrint, in

43. Finished and unfinished products from a glass workshop excavated at Comacchio (Universita Ca' Foscari – Venice).

44. Settlements in the Venice lagoon began developing like Comacchio between the 5th and 8th centuries. Torcello, in the northern part of the lagoon, was one of the oldest Venetian sites. Today, a view towards Venice from the bell tower of the Cathedral of Santa Maria Assunta, established in the 7th century, gives an idea of how these early settlements must have looked (Photo: Athena Trakadas).

modern Albania, for example, was an ancient city that had become little more than a village in the early medieval period. In the 9th century, after being controlled briefly by the Bulgars, it became an outpost of the Byzantine Empire.[10] There are, for example, other locations which provide more evidence, such as Malta. Here, amphorae dating to the 8th and 9th centuries from southern Italy, the Aegean and the Crimea are found. These finds are not possible to understand if associated only with local consumption on Malta – they are perhaps better explained if the island is seen to function as an emporium in the trade between East and West.[11]

Until the first quarter of the 8th century, the island of Sicily seems to have been involved in local and long-distance exchange, with a strong circulation of goods within a system governed by *Patrimonium Sancti Petri*, whereby the Church of Rome controlled properties on the island. After the confiscation of these properties under the Byzantine emperor Leo III in the mid 8th century, and especially by the Islamic conquest of the entire island by 965, the situation changes. Then, the connections with the East and southern Italy seem to remain, at least for part of the island, albeit at a lower level than the previous centuries.[12]

Up to the time that Theodosios visited Venice in the 9th century, the direct relationship of the lagoonal city with the western Mediterranean seems modest. Venice's relationship with the East is also not so clear at this time; in the eastern Mediterranean, there was a mix of Caliphate- and Byzantine-controlled territories and maritime activities – some commercial, some piratical. Like in the Baltic, hoards of *dinars* and *dirhams* have been found in Venice and some from Torcello, but it is likely that they were brought there by traders who were not from the Muslim caliphates, as these groups did not seem to penetrate the Adriatic at this time.[13]

45. One of Comacchio's products: the matrix for a glass cameo (right, 4.5 × 2.8 cm) and a finished glass cameo (left) from an excavated workshop in the city (Universita Ca' Foscari – Venice).

UFUK KOCABAŞ

Constantinople's Byzantine harbour: the Yenikapı excavations

At the very heart of the imperial Byzantine capital, Constantinople, was its relationship to the sea. Straddling the Bosporus, on the narrow waterway that connects the Black Sea to the Sea of Marmara and eventually the Mediterranean, the city needed harbours for the vessels that facilitated the trade, supply, and communication routes throughout its realm. Various kinds of raw materials and food were brought to the city, first arriving to its harbours. And from these harbours, cargo ships left with trade goods, galleys of the empire's navy sailed out to protect the Byzantine waterways, and imperial administrators like the *patrikios* Theodosios departed on diplomatic missions. There is no doubt that the importance of maintaining a relationship to the sea for the well-being of Constantinople also had an impact on the growing political power of the Byzantine emperors, who built several harbours for the city.

The modern city of Istanbul continues to require new transportation connections, and on the shoreline in the district of Yenikapı, a Marmaray and Metro railway hub station was recently constructed. In November 2004, Istanbul Archaeological Museums initiated a collaborative archaeological salvage excavation at Yenikapı, on the European side of the Bosporus, several kilometres south-west of the heart of ancient Constantinople. This salvage operation turned out to be the greatest archaeological research projects in the city's history: over 58,000 m² of one of the most important Byzantine harbours of the city, the *Portus Theodosiacus*, or Harbour of the Emperor Theodosius, was excavated.[1]

The harbour was named after the Byzantine emperor Theodosius I

46. Modern Istanbul, like its predecessor Constantinople, spans the Bosporus – the narrow waterway that connects the Black Sea to the Mediterranean (Photo: Athena Trakadas).

47. The Byzantine *Portus Theodosiacus* was excavated in Istanbul in preparation for the city's new metro line development. Harbour structures like stone quays, shown here, were found along with shipwrecks (© Istanbul University Yenikapı Shipwrecks Project Archive).

(r. 379-395 CE), and was established at the mouth of Lykos stream, which flowed through the then-walled city and emptied into the Sea of Marmara. It is now clear from these excavations that the earlier Eleutherios Harbour, which dates to the reign of Constantine I in the early 4th century, preceded the Theodosian Harbour.[2]

The recent excavations have shown that the harbour was used until the 11th century, when alluvial deposits from the Lykos stream filled in the basin. Fortunately, these deposits buried thousands of artefacts that have shed new light on the daily life, religion, trade, and technology of the early medieval period. Different types of amphorae and tablewares, coins, candles, figurines, leather sandals, ornaments and a large number of nautical artefacts – including rigging equipment such as pulleys, ropes, and toggles, and also stone and iron anchors – have been unearthed by the museum's ongoing archaeological salvage project. Among the most significant finds are 37 shipwrecks that constitute the largest medieval shipwreck collection ever found at a single site.[3]

Contemporary texts tell us that there were two granaries in the east section of the harbour, *Horrea Alexandrina* and *Horrea Theodosiana*, indicating that it was a commercial harbour specifically for ships loaded with mass cargoes of grain from Alexandria, in Egypt.[4] Strong winds and currents at the Dardanelles, at the western entrance of the Sea of Marmara, would cause these ships to wait for safer weather conditions. In order to avoid such delays, granaries were built on Tenedos Island in the northeastern Aegean by the Emperor Justinian (r. 527-565). Thus bigger sea-going ships unloaded their cargoes here while smaller ships shuttled through the Sea of Marmara to the Byzantine capital. These Egyptian grain ships supplied Constantinople until the Umayyad Caliphate's conquest of Egypt on 641 ended this route.

In addition to the grain trade, construction materials such as marble from the island of Proconnesos, tiles, bricks, and timber were shipped in by sea. Other food supplies, such as fruits and wine, were brought to the Theodosian Harbour to meet the growing demands of the population of Constantinople.[5]

A number of the ships that transported these goods have been found at the site and are undergoing study by a team from Istanbul University's Department of Conservation of Marine Archaeological Objects.[6] According to preliminary studies, the Yenikapı shipwrecks can be basically divided in two groups. The first group is represented by cargo ships of various dimensions dating from 5th to 10th centuries. These ships had flat bottom sections and rounded hulls and carried a single sail, probably a lateen, placed towards the bow. On the basis of their relatively small size, averaging 8-10 m in length with some slightly larger, most of the ships would have been used over short distances, and a few ships would have functioned as simple fishing vessels. These might have been locally built, with wood analyses showing that they were constructed of oak, pine, chestnut, and ash – common in the western and northern Anatolian region. However, the wide distribution of these wood species throughout the Mediterranean makes it far from certain that Yenikapı was the home port of the ships.[7]

At least four of the cargo ships were found with the cargoes still on board, but the reasons for their sinking has not yet been clarified.[8] The rest of the ships found without cargoes, anchors and rigging equipment were probably vessels abandoned in the harbour after a long period of service.[9]

Six galleys or oared vessels constitute the second group of Yenikapı shipwrecks. There were no original contemporary examples of this type prior to the Yenikapı excavations and the information on this type of early medieval vessel was previously limited to literary sources. These first archaeological examples of galleys show quite different hull forms than the cargo ships. They are ca 25 m long, with narrow hulls that must have been designed for speed and manoeuvrability.[10] The Yenikapı galleys likely belong to the *galea* type mentioned in Byzantine texts and these would have served the Byzantine navy as scout vessels escorting *dromōns*, the main type of rowed warship of the Byzantine Empire.[11]

Due to a thick layer of muddy sediment, the Yenikapı shipwrecks were found in a relatively better condition compared to other wrecks found in Mediterranean waters. However, regardless of their fair condition, it is not possible to store or display any waterlogged ship timbers in a museum without conservation and restoration procedures. This is currently being undertaken, through the cleaning of the timbers and chemical conservation techniques. Afterwards, the ship timbers will be re-assembled, making it possible for future public exhibition.[12]

(© Istanbul University Yenikapı Shipwrecks Project Archive)

48. *Urbis Constantinopolitanae Delineatio*, one of the oldest views of Constantinople published in 1422 by Cristoforo de Buondelmonti of Florence. The area where *Portus Theodosiacus* was located is circled at the mouth of the Lykos stream (after Kocabaş 2008: Map 3).

49. One of the finds from the Yenikapı site include the Yenikapı 35 wreck, the remains of a 5th-century cargo ship shown here during excavation.

The Yenikapı salvage excavations have revealed a wealth of archaeological material dating from the early medieval period in the eastern Mediterranean. The 37 shipwrecks uncovered date from the 5th to 10th centuries, and this wide chronology provides a unique opportunity to understand the development of shipbuilding traditions and technologies in the Mediterranean.

Although the results are preliminary, there are many new construction details that have been discovered, helping clarify the transition for and reasons behind "shell-based" to "frame-based" shipbuilding techniques in the broader Mediterranean.

In addition, the unique finds of the trade goods and features of the Theodosian Harbour – from stone quays to wooden pilings for docks – provide a unique window into the construction of and daily life within a major Byzantine port. This is especially unique due to the level of preservation caused by the sedimentation of the Lykos stream, and the lack of study of other similar harbour sites, many of which lie still undiscovered under major cities.

50. Items used for commercial activities were also found in the harbour excavations at Yenikapı. Examples include a weight likely manufactured in the city, similar to this one in brown-green glass from the 7th century. An inscription in Greek, "of Addaeos" possibly names its owner. Ca 16 mm diameter, 1.16 g (© Trustees of the British Museum).

51. Nautical artefacts were also found during excavations at Yenikapı. Stone anchors, similar to this ca 45 cm-high three-holed example found off the coast of southern Turkey (now in the Amphora Müzesi in Taşucu) have been discovered. Crosses were also sometimes carved into these ship parts (Photo: Athena Trakadas).

ATHENA TRAKADAS

A sea in transition: ships of the Mediterranean

52. Cargo ships of the 9th century had closely-spaced frames, like those on the Bozburun wreck, pictured during excavation off the west coast of Turkey. The cargo was wine amphorae from the Crimea (© Institute of Nautical Archaeology).

The 9th-century Mediterranean was a maritime world in transition. The Mediterranean of the earlier Roman Empire can be characterised as a rather homogenous sea, the *Mare Nostrum*, linked by relative political, cultural and economic stability from coast to coast. Five or so centuries later, the Mediterranean of the 9th century had become a mixed sea of maritime spheres shared and contended among a variety of states, economies and religions: the Byzantine or Eastern Roman Empire and the Frankish Empire along the Mediterranean's northern shores with emerging polities like Venice in between, and the Umayyad and Abbasid Caliphates along the Mediterranean's western, southern and eastern shores. When Theodosios voyaged from Constantinople to Venice in 840 CE, the peoples of this mixed sea sometimes crossed and challenged these various maritime spheres for trade or in conflict. The vessels they used shared some similarities with ships of the Baltic and Indian Ocean world but possessed their own unique characteristics that reflected advancements in a long tradition of Mediterranean shipbuilding technology.

Contemporary illustrations and texts provide a glimpse of the ships and boats that plied the Mediterranean's waters in the 9th century. Images of ships at this time are few, due to cultural beliefs and periods of iconoclasm. They mainly derive from the Byzantine sphere of influence and are relegated to unclear graffiti and illuminated manuscripts – which at this time, like the well-known *Homilies of St. Gregory of Nazianzus* (ca 880), show only very stylised boats for the sake of narration or repeat artistic standards that could be centuries old. Texts from this period provide some information, but due to their intended message or audience, can be too generalised and leave out important details. But for the early centuries of the Islamic caliphates' presence in the Mediterranean, texts – such as those from the Cairo Genizah (a store-room for texts in a synagogue) – form our main source of information on ships and maritime activities.[1]

Archaeological finds of ships from this period therefore serve as the best references for understanding the types, sizes, propulsion and methods of construction of galleys and especially cargo ships. A handful of shipwrecks from the 9th century, of varying levels of preservation, are known;[2] thanks to the ground-breaking excavations at Yenikapı, the *Portus Theodosiacus* of Constantinople, 10 wrecks have recently revealed a great deal more about vessels used within the Byzantine Empire at this time.[3] But at present, ships belonging to other cultures and states of the 9th-century Mediterranean world remain relatively unknown archaeologically.

However, texts such as *On the capture of Thessalonica* by Ioannis Kameniates (fl. 10th century), *Chronographia* by Theophanes (d. 818), the Aphrodito Papyri from Egypt (early 8th century), and *Kitab Futūh al-buldān* ('Book of the Conquests of the Lands') by al-Balādhurī (d. 892) suggest that ships belonging to the early Islamic caliphates likely did not differ greatly from other vessels on the Mediterranean. When the Umayyad Caliphate began to expand along the eastern coasts of the Mediterranean in the mid 7th century, local ships, ship yards and shipwrights – specifically mentioned as 'Greeks and Copts' – were conscripted. Despite the lack of archaeological evidence for vessels outside the Byzantine world, these documented acts of appropriation indicate that Mediterranean vessels, at least in the first few centuries after the arrival of Islam into the region, likely remained relatively homogenous in appearance and construction.[4]

Like the communities and politics of the Mediterranean, methods of ship construction were also in transition. Shipwrights built within a range of techniques that they knew. Generally, like their counterparts in the Baltic and Indian Ocean, Mediterranean ships did not have transoms, and clear fore and aft shapes were created by stem- and stern-posts that joined to the keel and formed a smooth curvature. A ship's hull was largely built of closely-spaced frames that dictated its shape and provided its major support, creating a slightly boxier cargo space. Planks, laid edge-to-edge, carvel-like, were attached to the frames with small iron nails or wooden treenails; sometimes the edges of the planks were joined to each other by small dowels or coaks. Through-beams often were set across a vessel's width on the sheer fore and aft to provide stability to the hull, and rear quarter steering rudders were set

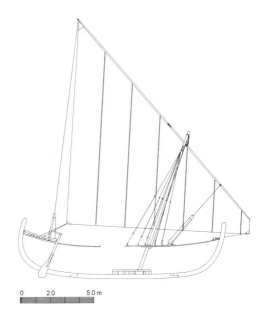

53. The Bozburun wreck reconstructed sail plan: a 15 m-long and 5 m-wide cargo ship of ca 30 tons with a lateen sail (Drawing: M. Harpster).

to both port and starboard. This type of construction differed from earlier methods, where more emphasis was placed on strengthening the hull shell itself, with planks joined to each other by a network of mortise and tenons or in some parts of the Mediterranean, sewn together, with the frames inserted at a later stage. These earlier "shell-based construction" methods gave way slowly to what can be seen in some of the 9th century ship-finds, often referred to by modern scholars as "frame-based construction" methods. Ships constructed following the later techniques used less labour-intensive methods and wood, and the overall building costs were reduced.[5]

Square sails, once standard on Mediterranean ships since the Bronze Age, became less and less common from the 5th and 6th centuries onwards – triangular lateen sails appear frequently alongside square sails in graffiti and mosaics, and are described in texts. By the 9th century, the square sail appears to have lost out in favour of the newer rig, and in the 12th century, seagoing ships in the Mediterranean used lateen sails almost universally. Their design was likely born out of experimentation by adjusting the yard of a square sail and manipulating its brails to form a triangle, inclined square or quadrilateral-shaped sail.[6]

Cargo ships of the 9th century, as demonstrated by those found at Yenikapı and elsewhere, like the Bozburun wreck (Bozburun, Turkey), or the Tantura B wreck (Dor, Israel), varied in size, but were generally between 10 to 15 m long.[7] They were broad in beam, and boxier in cross-section, in order to accommodate their cargoes. In most cases it is assumed they were decked only at the bow and stern, to provide easy access to the hold during on- and off-loading. In Byzantine Greek texts small vessels could be called *naus*, *ploîon*, *skafos*, *holkas*, *karabos*, *agraion*, *sandalion* and *akreisandalion* – some of these terms simply imply 'boat'.[8] Larger vessels began to appear in texts by the late 8th century: *pragmateutika*, *emporeutika*, and rarely, *karaboploïa* (the Greek indicating the vessel's purpose: *pragma*- 'thing' or 'goods'; *empor*- 'commercial' or 'mercantile').[9] Typical cargo ships in the Mediterranean were called *qārib* or *markab* in Arabic, but these terms could also refer to any type of boat, small or large.[10]

54. The Yenikapı 12 wreck, shown during excavation, was carrying wine amphorae from the Crimea – similar to the Bozburun wreck. It sank in the *Portus Theodosiacus* sometime in the 9th century (© Istanbul University Yenikapı Shipwrecks Project Archive).

The Byzantine war galley, the *galea* or *dromōn* (from the Greek *dramein*, 'to run' or 'move quickly') is first mentioned in the late 5th century.[11] At this time, it is understood to have been a long and narrow ship with a single row of oars, open or partially decked, possibly with a single sail. Beginning in the 7th century, nearly identical galleys were used by Mediterranean navies of the caliphates. Texts reveal that in Arabic, *safina* or *shīnī* were galley types; smaller one-masted vessels were called *shakhturs* and *ghurāb*; *shelandi* or *markab shelandi* refer to a fully-decked warships.[12]

The 9th and 10th centuries saw the development of Mediterranean fleets of larger galleys with two rows of oars, several sails, and experimentation with flaming projectiles. These larger ships were called *ousiakos*, *pamphylion* and *chelandrion* in Byzantine texts.[13] *Chelandrion* (pl. *chelandria*) were the largest *dromōns*, but this word was also synonymous with *dromōn* by the 10th century.[14] Called *zalandriae* in Italian, it was the construction of this type that Theodosios, as part of his naval responsibilities as *Chartoularios tou Bestiariou*, might have overseen in Venice in 840.[15] A treatise on how to construct a *dromōn*, based on a much earlier source, was commissioned in the 10th century by the *patrikios* and *parakoimomenos* (Grand Chamberlain) Basil, and until the excavations of those at Yenikapı, no archaeological examples of *galeas* or *dromōns* were known.[16] Now it is possible to see that ca 25–30 m-long galleys were similar in their overall methods of construction to cargo ships, but were designed to be fast vessels transporting troops instead of trade goods.[17]

In the 9th century, the new mixture of cultures, religions and economies impacted the Mediterranean maritime world – how and where transport at sea was undertaken and the vessels that sailed such voyages. Cargo ships were generally smaller than their Roman predecessors, with lateen sails, and well suited for use by the increasing number of independent merchants who traded within and between the shores of the early Byzantine Empire, the caliphates and the numerous small emerging polities like Venice. Lighter galleys were rapidly deployable and manoeuvrable, enabling naval fleets for defence against a myriad of states that lined the Mediterranean. These changes were made possible by the development of more economical ship construction methods that remained standard in the Mediterranean world for centuries afterwards.

55. Galleys were relatively unknown archaeologically until the excavations undertaken at Yenikapı, in Istanbul. Shown here is the well-preserved Yenikapı 16 galley wreck, dating from the mid 8th century (© Istanbul University Yenikapı Shipwrecks Project Archive).

IŞIL ÖZAİT-KOCABAŞ

The Yenikapı 12 wreck: connecting Constantinople

The so-called "Yenikapı 12 shipwreck" was one of the 37 shipwrecks discovered during the excavations at Yenikapı in Istanbul, Turkey.[1] Based on a coin found inside the wreck, it is dated to the 9th century; results of radiocarbon testing of the wood from the boat gives a date range between 672–870 CE.[2]

Yenikapı 12 was an approximately 9.60 m-long, 2.60 m-wide trading vessel. It had a single lateen sail and was steered by two quarter-rudders, characteristic of Mediterranean ships of the period. It had a special compartment at the stern, and a foredeck, side-deck, and poop deck. The ship's wide design in the bow and midships, as well as low-profile frames increased its cargo capacity.[3]

Old and new technology were used together in the construction of this small cargo vessel: it represents a phase in the transition from "shell-based construction" to "frame-based construction", and proves that the earlier "shell-based construction technique" was not forgotten by 9th-century shipwrights.[4]

The wreck's cargo consists of both complete and broken amphorae. The captain's personal belongings were also found in a special compartment in the aft of the vessel: a brazier and its lid used for cooking, a cooking pot, mugs and jugs, glass goblet sherds, and two amphorae placed beneath the rest. These finds are significant as they provide information on the home port of the ship and the nationalities of the captain and crew. In particular, the amphorae in the captain's compartment are from the Crimea, suggesting a relationship between

56. The Yenikapı 12 shipwreck during excavations in Istanbul (© Istanbul University Yenikapı Shipwrecks Project Archive).

57. Liquid cargoes like wine were often transported in ceramic amphorae, like this type, ca 40 cm high, manufactured in the Crimea, in the northern Black Sea. The type has been found at 9th-century port sites in Istanbul, the Aegean, and the Adriatic (Tauric Chersoneses Museum, Ukraine, NPTC. No. 3290).

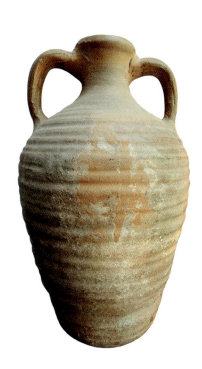

58. Small 9th-century cargo ships like the Yenikapı 12 shipwreck, shown here reconstructed, had two quarter rudders, an open hold and a lateen sail (© Istanbul University Yenikapı Shipwrecks Project Archive).

the Yenikapı 12 ship and the Black Sea. Knowledge of the last route of the ship will only be available when the evaluation of the amphorae and their contents is finalised, however. But the wood used to build the ship – chestnut, ash, oak species, walnut and hornbeam – comes from northern Anatolia.

At the time Yenikapı 12 sailed into what was then the Theodosian Harbour in Constantinople in the 9th century, some of the Byzantine Empire's maritime trade had shifted northwards. The Black Sea's economy and trade was beginning to revive, and this drew Byzantine traders to the region;[5] it was at this time too that Theodosios set sail from the city, and possibly even this port, on his mission to Venice and the West.

THEODOSIOS' WORLD   87

59. The seal belonging to the *patrikios* Theodosios found at Ribe, Denmark. Dating from the mid 9th century, this lead seal is about 3 cm in diameter, and would have sealed his diplomatic letters (Museums of Southwest Jutland, Denmark).

60. Theodosios' seals from Tissø (left) and Hedeby (centre and right), ca 3 cm in diameter. The Hedeby example was made using another *boulloterion* (National Museum of Denmark, Danish Prehistory / Stiftung Schleswig-Holsteinische Landes-museen Schloss Gottorf, Wikinger-museum Haithabu, Germany).

JONATHAN SHEPARD & J.-C. CHEYNET

The seals of Theodosios

Altogether four seals of a *Chartoularios tou Bestiariou* ('Chief Secretary to the (Imperial) Stores and Treasury') called Theodosios are known: one now at the Archaeological Museum in Istanbul, the others unearthed in Denmark and in Germany. Their inscriptions do not mention Baboutzikos, the family name of the envoy who was despatched abroad by the Emperor Theophilos in the 9th century, according to Byzantine chronicles.[1] But they dub him *patrikios*, the court-title certainly held by Theodosios Baboutzikos. *Patrikios* was very senior, unlikely to have belonged to two persons called Theodosios simultaneously, and the head of the *Bestiarion* was customarily a *patrikios* in the mid 9th century. The seals' characteristics are consistent with this era, and the envoy of the chronicles almost certainly issued the seals. Byzantine officials of rank had their own seals, stating their name, office and title(s). They signalled their status, devotion to the empire and piety: many seals show a saint, the Mother of God, or a cross,[2] and Theodosios' are no exception.

The three seals from Northern Europe came to light during excavations at Hedeby (Germany) and at Ribe and a manor beside Lake Tissø (Denmark).[3] The seal in Istanbul's Archaeological Museum was probably found in the city or nearby. Theodosios could have sent it back while on assignment, or it might simply register his activities in the empire's capital, Constantinople.

The Ribe example On one side (left, above) within a circle of stylised foliage, a cruciform monogram containing in its quadrants the usual Byzantine formula for invoking the Virgin Mary (Type Laurent V):

Ṭω – Cω – Δω – .ω

Θεοτόκε βοήθει τῷ σῷ δού[λ]ῳ

('Mother of God, help thy servant')

On the other side (the reverse) an inscription of four lines, surmounted

and preceded by a miniature cross, and followed by a miniature cross set amongst florets:

+ΘΕΟΔΟ|..ΩΠΑΤΡΙΚ/Β|
..ΠΑ/SΧΑΡ/Τ.|ΒΕСΤΙΑ.|+

Θεοδο[σί]ῳ πατρικ(ίῳ) β(ασιλικῷ) [(πρωτο)σ]πα(θαρίῳ) (καὶ) χαρ(τουλαρίῳ) τ[οῦ] βεστιαρ(ίου)]

('Theodosios, *patrikios*, imperial *protospatharios* and *Chartoularios* of the *Bestiarion*')

The Tissø seal is not well preserved but has, on the reverse, the same inscription as that on the Ribe example. The design of the Hedeby example is very similar to the above, but the inscription has an extra 'Y' in *protospatharios*. The inscription of the seal from Istanbul is that of the Ribe and Tissø examples, but we can tell it was struck from another *boulloterion* by the different positioning of the individual letters. So altogether three *boulloteria* were used to make the four known examples of Theodosios' seals. The shape of several letters suggests a dating to the first half of the 9th century. For example, the letter 'B' has horizontal strokes – serifs – whereas in the 8th century its serifs were usually oblique. Conversely, the closed 'B' of our seals was going out of fashion, yet still occurs on seals of Theodosios' contemporaries, such as a Thracian customs-officer in 831/32 CE.[4]

Striking a seal was done with an iron *boulloterion*, an implement resembling a pair of pincers with disc-shaped jaws, upon which were engraved images or, as upon Theodosios' seals, inscriptions. To make a seal, one placed a lead blank between the jaws and then struck with a hammer, forcing the jaws together.[5] Besides imprinting the inscriptions, this served to close a hollow channel running through the blank; a cord was run along the channel, and hammering the jaws together served to lock in the two ends of the cord. The cord was attached to a document, keeping its contents secret until delivery to the recipient, who would cut the cord.[6]

We cannot be sure that all the seals reached their intended destination. The documents they authenticated were letters, almost certainly in Greek, the language of the seals' inscriptions, but Byzantine emissaries commonly amplified the contents of the letters they delivered, making proposals too sensitive to put in writing. Besides sealing messages, lead seals could also be attached to bags full of gold coins, or to other gifts for the 'barbarians' or non-Christian neighbours.[7] Quite how much gold was given would depend on an emissary's assessment of individual recipients and their potential usefulness, whereas sealed purses would have had more limited impact. Indeed, *nomismata* (coins) of Theophilos found at Hedeby and Gnezdovo (near Smolensk in present-day Russia)[8] could reflect gift-giving on the part of Theodosios Baboutzikos' well-stocked emissaries.

HELLE HORSNÆS

Theophilos' coin: treasure and image

During Emperor Theophilos' rule (813–842 CE) the Byzantine Empire had gained strength and stood at its strongest point since the Muslim conquests in the 7th century. Based in Constantinople, he controlled an army and navy which fought in the Mediterranean, the Balkans and the Middle East. His diplomats, of whom Theodosios was one, were active from the Rhine to Mesopotamia.

The obverse of Theophilos' gold coin (*solidus*), minted between 829–842, shows the emperor dressed conventionally in a sleeved tunic (*dalmatic*) covered by a cloak (*clamys*) that is fastened on the right shoulder with an elaborate pin. His hair and beard are trimmed, and he wears a diadem decorated with a cross, the forerunner of a crown. He holds the imperial insignia, the long cross and the so-called *akakia* – a cylinder containing dust that symbolised the mortality of man. These all reveal his status as reigning Christian emperor. On the reverse are portraits of his father, Michael II (r. 820-829) and his little son Constan-

61. Theophilos' gold coin (*solidus*) is only ca 2 cm in diameter. The obverse is shown on the left, with the reverse on the right (National Museum of Denmark, The Royal Collection of Coins and Medals).

tine, who died at a tender age. They are dressed as the emperor, but do not hold the insignia.

The might of Byzantine emperors rested on gold. Coinage dwindled in Western Europe after the decline of the Western Roman Empire during the 5th century, but the Roman monetary system continued to prevail in the Byzantine Empire. Gold had been introduced as the basic unit already by Roman emperor Constantine the Great in the early 4th century, and the high denomination issues in gold were supplemented by large amounts of small coin struck in bronze for daily use. Silver coins were generally struck on a smaller scale.[1]

Although contacts between the Byzantine Empire and the West were not completely broken off, finds of Byzantine gold coins from the 8th–9th centuries are rare throughout Central and Western Europe.[2] They mainly derive from princely contexts or from communication hubs as Hedeby, where a Byzantine gold coin of Theophilos, re-worked into jewellery, was found in a grave.[3] These coins are generally believed to be the remnants of gold brought to Western Europe as diplomatic gifts or political payments.[4] Although rare, the influx of these coins left their mark: the characteristic facing portrait of Byzantine emperors became a prototype on some coinages of Central Europe as well as Scandinavia.

NETWORKS

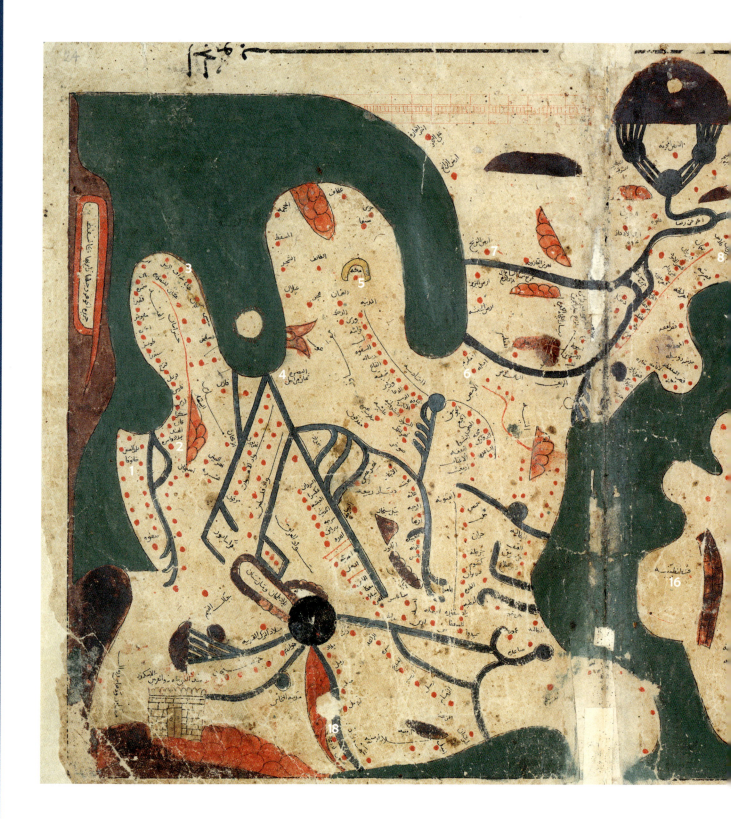

94 NETWORKS

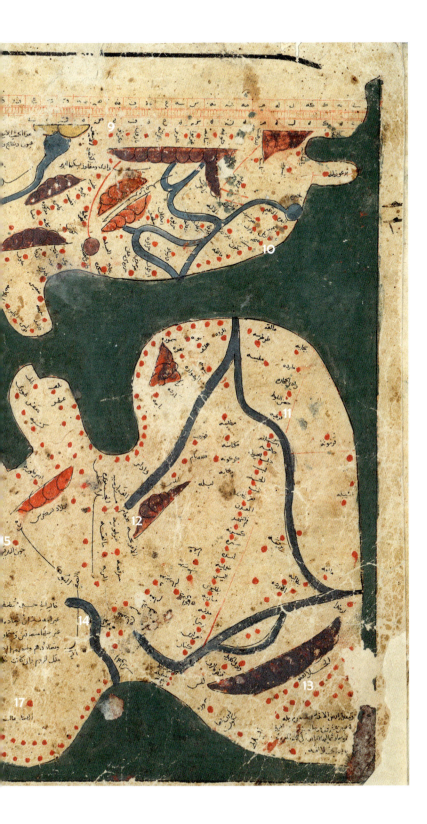

62. A map of the world in *The Book of Curiosities of the Sciences and Marvels for the Eyes*. The Arabic treatise was first compiled in Egypt before 1050 CE, with this manuscript copy made in Egypt or Greater Syria in the late 12th or early 13th centuries. The map accompanies Book 2, Chapter 2, "On the Depiction of the Earth", and is oriented with south at the top and north at the bottom. It shows representations of Africa, Asia and Europe and the seas in between – with parts of the Mediterranean, Atlantic, Baltic, Caspian and Black Seas combined. The map extends from present-day China (far left) to the Atlantic coast of Spain and Morocco (far right), and from Ukraine and Turkey (bottom) to Mali and Tanzania (top) (The Bodleian Libraries, University of Oxford. MS. Arab. C. 90, fol. 24a–23b: Book 2, Chapter 2).

1 *Balad al-Ṣīn*: China
2 *Al-Hind*: India
3 *Siraf*
4 *Al-Baṣrah*: Basra
5 *Makkah*: Mecca
6 *Aylah*
7 *Arḍ al-Zanj*: Land of the Zanj
8 *Al-Qayrawān*: Kairouan
9 *K.znū*: Gao (Mali)
10 *Ṭanjah*: Tangier
11 *Qurḍubah*: Cordoba
12 *Al-Ifranjah*: the Franks
13 *Al-Jallāliqah*: Galicia (Spain)
14 *Al-Ṣaqālibah*: the Slavs
15 *Jūn al-Bārqīq*: Gulf of the Venetians
16 *Qusṭanṭiniyah*: Constantinople
17 *Al-Kūmān*: Kiev
18 *Adharbayjān*: Azerbaijan

NETWORKS 95

UNN PEDERSEN

Kaupang: Viking-Age expansion to the North

Around 890 CE Ohthere the seafarer arrived by ship at Kaupang in Skiringssal – a small town by the outlet of the Oslo Fjord, in present-day Norway. This was more than one month's sailing south from his home in Hålogaland, "if one camped at night and each day had favourable wind", as stated in his report.[1]

The report provides no information on Ohthere's length of stay or whereabouts at Kaupang. The place merely serves as a fixed point on his route, but hints of what he might have experienced are provided by recent archaeological excavations.[2] He came to a settlement by the shore characterised by trade, craft activities and daily life – established on the initiative of a Danish king almost a century earlier. Drifting through narrow streets he could have witnessed glass bead production and visited workshops where jewellery and dress items were being produced. He could have admired newly cast brooches, neatly decorated with animal ornaments and made of shiny brass, a raw material brought

63. Swords, spearheads, axe, arrowhead, stirrups, parts of a harness and boat rivets from man's grave at Kaupang, Norway. Iron, ca 850–950 CE (Photo: Eirik Irgens Johnsen, Museum of Cultural History, University of Oslo).

to Kaupang by long-distance trade.³ Along with nearby farmers and traders in a maritime network he could have acquired exotic commodities from the Middle East, the Mediterranean and the Frankish Empire.

The waterfront settlement was part of a larger complex, comprising large cemeteries, an aristocratic hall building, a "thing" meeting site and a sacred lake. At the cemeteries we find some of the persons of Kaupang who would have welcomed wealthy guests from afar, like Ohthere. A large burial

64. Cord tightener of whale bone, perhaps used for a tent. From man's grave at Kaupang, Norway, ca 10 cm long, ca 850–950 CE (Photo: Eirik Irgens Johnsen, Museum of Cultural History, University of Oslo).

mound on Kaupang's outskirts illustrates the life of such a man of high social standing in coastal Norway, who was buried in the early 9th century.⁴

The cremation grave – the wealthiest grave excavated at Kaupang – contains a set of weapons: a sword, a spear, an axe, a shield boss and two arrows. Accordingly the buried person is interpreted as a man by archaeologists, and he is presented as a warrior by the ones who survived him. Wealth is demonstrated by the quantity of the grave goods, but also the quality as demonstrated by the sword: the hilt has remains of inlays of silver and copper alloys, and the blade is decorated with several crosses and the inscription *Ulfbert*. This was the famous trade mark of a Frankish sword smithy.

The man may have been buried in a boat, like many others in Scandinavia at the time, but a collection of iron nails is all that is left of such a vessel.

The boat graves suggest that many people identified with seafaring in life and in death. A pair of stirrups demonstrates that the man was a horseman travelling over land too, and a horse bit and a rattle suggest that the horse may have been buried with him. A possible cord tightener for a tent and a chest for storing personal items similarly allude to travelling.

The cord tightener is made of whale bone, one of the materials mentioned by Ohthere as a resource from the North. The grave contains tools well suited for the working of bone, antler and wood: a rasp, a spoon auger, a whetstone and a knife. We can only speculate on how the whale bone ended up at Kaupang. The horseman might have obtained the raw material on a trip up north; but it could also have been brought by a character like Ohthere, travelling to market from the far north.

MATEUSZ BOGUCKI

Truso, silver and trade

La ilāha illā Allāh wahdahū lā sharīka lahū ('There is no god but God alone. He has no associate') is the most common religious invocation known from the whole Viking world. But it is doubtful if any of the Scandinavians, Slavs or Balts who had heard or seen it written could understand its meaning. This text appears on *dirhams* – silver coins from the 8th to 10th centuries, which were imported from the Islamic caliphates through Russia, Central Europe and Scandinavia to the northern lands of Europe in millions of copies.[1] In the emporium Truso, located in Janów Pomorski on the east bank of the Vistula Estuary in northeast Poland, more than 1,000 such coins and fragments have been found.

Truso was first described by the English sailor Wulfstan in the 880s CE, in the same book which preserved Ohthere's description of the North.[2] Truso existed as an international trading place from ca 800 to ca 950 and covered over 20 hectares. Excavations have revealed traces of many crafts, including iron working, the production of gold and silver ornaments, bronze casting, comb making, glass working, weaving and boat building. Close to the harbour there was a trading quarter, as shown by the concentration of finds of coins and weights.[3]

As in any other long-distance trade, merchants had to diversify their portfolios, but, according to a number of written sources, the most important objects of trade were slaves. At the caliphs' courts and at the palaces of the aristocracy and nobleman, slaves worked, served and gave birth to new generations of both slaves and free people. The number of East European slaves in the Abbasid Caliphate was very high – already in 812/3 the poet al-Tabari wrote that the streets of Baghdad were full of *al-jarādīja as-Saqāliba* – 'slavic locusts'.[4] Truso almost certainly was an important point in this slave market network to the East.

The *dirhams* that came into the Baltic had relatively high value. The Spanish Sephardic Jewish traveller Ibrāhīm ibn Ya'qūb (al-Tartushi), who visited Mainz, Hedeby, Prague and Rome in the 960s, notes that in Prague for one *dirham* coin he could buy 10 chickens.[5] This explains in some way why most of the coins found in Scandinavia or in Slavic areas are cut into pieces. Silver could be used also by its weight[6] – hundreds of balance weights and thousands of standardised weights are recorded from Viking-Age settlements. Apart from silver, other means of payment were almost certainly used – glass beads (most of them imported from the Islamic caliphates), furs, salt, iron, and – last but not least – the gold of the North, amber.

Truso was also one of the most important trading sites for amber. To date more than 30 kg, which means several thousand fragments of raw amber, workshop refuse and finished objects have been found, including two amber hoards, one of which weighed almost 10 kg. Baltic amber was valued in the Mediterranean and Near East for centuries before the Viking Age. The stone was called *kahraba* in Arabic.

65. *Dirham* coins from the Islamic caliphates found at Truso (Janów Pomorski), Poland. Silver, ca 2 cm in diameter, ca 800–950 CE (Photo: Leszek Okoński, Collection of the Museum of Archaeology and History in Elbląg, photo archive).

66. Weights from Truso (Janów Pomorski) in Poland. Iron plated and copper alloy, ca 800–950 CE (Photo: Leszek Okoński, Collection of the Museum of Archaeology and History in Elbląg, photo archive).

67. Semi-precious stones and glass beads from Truso (Janów Pomorski) in Poland. Rock crystal, carnelian and glass, ca 800–950 CE (Photo: Leszek Okoński, Collection of the Museum of Archaeology and History in Elbląg, photo archive).

68. Necklace made of amber from Truso (Janów Pomorski), Poland, ca 800–950 CE (Photo: Leszek Okoński, Collection of the Museum of Archaeology and History in Elbląg, photo archive).

According to al-Bīrūnī, Baltic amber was better than Chinese amber, and peoples from present-day Turkistan used it as an amulet against evil forces. Ibn Ğazzār from Kairouan in present-day Tunisia notes that amber was also called "Baltic lighthouse".[7] From the 12th century there are reports that Baltic amber was traded even to China.

Vikings became key actors on this silver, slave, fur and amber trade between North and South. To make this trade more effective, they took part in establishing numerous trading posts across the Baltic region, including Truso.

NETWORKS

CHRIS LOWE

The Inchmarnock 'Hostage Stone'

A Scandinavian sailor in the 9th century, such as Ohthere, would know for good reason the point along the coast of Norway where "to starboard will be first Ireland", and then other islands in the Irish Sea and along the northern coasts of Scotland.[1] Around the Irish Sea at this time, many small kingdoms competed for power, and hostages and slaves were regularly taken. When Scandinavian sailors and warriors arrived in the late 8th century, slave raids intensified. Dublin was founded by Scandinavian Vikings in the 9th century as an important trading centre, and historical evidence indicates one of the commodities traded were slaves.[2] Whilst local chieftains and abbots might be seized for their value as ransom, clearly others were taken to be sold as slaves. The Scandinavian North – including Iceland – was a key market for slaves, but they were also sold to the western Umayyad Caliphate, in present-day Spain and Portugal:[3] a slave who was taken overseas, far from

69. The 'Hostage Stone', decorated stone slab from Inchmarnock, Scotland. Slate, 18 × 12 cm, ca 8th or 9th century (National Museum of Scotland/Bute Museum).

his homeland and culture, would be less likely to escape.

An inscribed beach stone found in an Early Christian monastery on the island of Inchmarnock, off Scotland's western coast, illustrates a part of this story. The flat, oval piece of slate is formed of two fragments. Essentially intact except for its upper right-hand and lower margins, the stone could have been held comfortably in the hand. Incised on the obverse are four human figures in profile, facing right: three warriors in chain-mail leading what appears to be a tied person to a sailing ship with 12 oars.[4] On the reverse, on a different alignment, are a series of letter-forms and a cruciform pattern. The epigraphy indicates an 8th- or 9th-century date. The style and proportions of the sketch indicate that it was probably made by a young child, presumably a novice from the monastic schoolhouse.

In light of the dates inferred from the epigraphic style, and the radiocarbon dates from the monastery site at Inchmarnock, which span the last quarter of the first millennium, it is possible that the image depicts a raiding party by a group of wild-haired Viking warriors. It is a familiar image also seen in the carved 'Doomsday scene' from the monastery of Lindisfarne in northeast England, with its group of axe- and sword-wielding warriors – usually identified as those same heathen warriors who, as recorded in the *Anglo-Saxon Chronicle* for 793, brought "rapine and slaughter" to Lindisfarne.[5]

According to the *Annals of Ulster*, compiled from contemporary sources, large numbers of Northumbrians, Britons and Picts were taken captive by Vikings and brought to Dublin in 871.[6] When Vikings sacked Armagh in 869, "ten thousand persons were lost between captives and slain". After this, the seizure of large numbers of captives by Vikings becomes a recurring feature of the Irish annals. In 881, Bárðr, the leader of the Dublin Vikings, sacked the church at Duleek and took its people captive. In 886, 280 people were seized at Kildare. In 895, 710 prisoners were rounded up at Armagh by Glúniarann and the Dublin Vikings. The systematic taking of captives continued through the 10th century. The sheer scale of these raiding parties is reflected in the *Annals of Ulster* for 950:

"Gothfrith Sigtryggsson with the Foreigners of Dublin plundered Kells, Donaghmore, Ardbracken, Dulane, Kilskyre, and other churches. They were all plundered from Kells. On this occasion, three thousand men or more were captured together with a great booty of cows and horses, of gold and silver."[7]

In addition to such reports, the stone from Inchmarnock provides a very personal glimpse, through the eyes of a child, of a time when Vikings and other seaborne raiders were an ever-present danger to island communities along the North's western seaways.

70. Decorative button produced in the British Isles, found in Aggersborg, Denmark. Copper alloy and enamel, ca 4 cm in diameter. Late 8th or 9th century (Dept. of Medieval and Renaissance Archaeology, Aarhus University).

71. Ringed pin found in Aggersborg, Denmark. The needle mimics the style of those from the British Isles. Iron, ca 11 cm long, 9th or 10th century (Dept. of Medieval and Renaissance Archaeology, Aarhus University).

SVEN KALMRING

Hedeby from the sea-side

72. A seaman's chest found in Hedeby's harbour. Oak and iron, 52 cm long, 10th century (Stiftung Schleswig-Holsteinische Landesmuseen Schloss Gottorf, Wikingermuseum Haithabu, Germany).

When the Norwegian merchant Ohthere reached the inner-most end of the 22 nautical mile-long Schlei fjord, one of the major maritime trading centres of the North, Hedeby, unfolded before his eyes. Having passed the administrative boundary of the harbour palisade he saw a waterfront which was densely lined with jetties and a wide range of trading vessels, warships and even logboats.[1] In the 890s CE the harbour was under development to meet the latest needs of large seagoing sailing ships, the likes of which Ohthere may have used. At this time, the harbour facilities were enlarged some 30 m out into the harbour basin. This effort in labour and timber was a vital investment for the trading centre so it could keep participating in long-distance maritime trade. Mooring there required a harbour due,[2] possibly collected by the king's reeve, the *comes vici*. As the harbour developed, individual facilities were partly merging into one common platform in front of Hedeby that also served as the town's market-place.

Witnesses of the vibrant harbour market are the goods that were lost during the on- and off-loading from ship to jetty, which disappeared into

the muddy water of the harbour basin.³ Trading connections to Norway are reflected by such finds as soapstone vessels from Østfold in eastern Norway and western Sweden, rod-formed whetstones, wheel stands and rotary whetstones made from Eidsborg schist from Telemark or dark schist from southwestern Norway, and even some reindeer antler used in comb production.⁴ Some of these artefacts might have even been among the commodities on Ohthere's ship when he called at Hedeby. As ca 40% of the Norwegian whetstones reached Hedeby as raw material, local craftsmen also manufactured whetstones on site. The impact of the maritime trade is also reflected further inland: soapstone and schist are distributed in the immediate hinterland of Hedeby.⁵ However it was not only commodities that were exchanged, but also ideas: aspects of boatbuilding and fishing techniques originating in the North Atlantic to some degree were adapted in the Schlei region.⁶

Ohthere experienced 9ᵗʰ-century Hedeby with its approximately 1,500 inhabitants⁷ as a cultural melting pot: he mentions Slavonic Wends, Saxons, Anglians and Danes here. Another important group, although not mentioned in his report to King Alfred, were the Frisians operating in the North Sea between Rhine Delta and England.⁸ Others came from even further places: recorded are the English merchant Wulfstan, the Icelandic warrior Gunnarr Hamundarson as well as the diplomats Ibrāhīm ibn Ya'qūb from Umayyad Cordoba and

73. Excavations in Hedeby's harbour in 1979/80 uncovered timbers from massive harbour facilities dating between 825–1010 CE (Stiftung Schleswig-Holsteinische Landesmuseen Schloss Gottorf, Wikingermuseum Haithabu, Germany).

Theodosios from Byzantine Constantinople or his messenger, as witnessed by the find of his seal.⁹

Even though there was a trading peace within the boundaries of the semi-circular town wall of Hedeby, crime was probably on the daily agenda, too. This is hard to prove through artefacts, however. But when a large part of Hedeby's harbour was excavated in 1979/80, more than 2,000 timbers and 1,600 post-holes from massive harbour facilities, plus a 31 m-long royal warship for an impressive crew of 54 to 62 persons were found. Among the small finds was a small oak seaman's chest found buried in the mud that also served as an individual rower's bench during his sea journeys.¹⁰ Its special form, with a wide base and narrower top, was developed to prevent it from tilting over in heavy seas. This chest once housed the most valuable possessions of a sailor in a small space of 52 × 23 × 27 cm, and was secured by a heavy iron lock. Likely sitting on the deck planks of his ship, the chest was ransacked, first by digging at the lock. In order to get rid of the evidence, the empty chest was thrown overboard, and weighted down with a stone from the ship's ballast, sank to the bottom of the harbour basin.

J.C. MOESGAARD & OLE KASTHOLM

Making new money: the Hedeby coin

During the first half of the 9th century, coins were a rare sight in Scandinavia. The trading town of Ribe had used its own coins for a century and around the year 800 individual foreign coins arrived in the country from its powerful neighbour in the south – the Frankish Empire – and from England. In the important trading centre at Hedeby in southern Jutland, the minting of coins began in the second quarter of the 9th century. Otherwise, coins were relatively unknown.[1]

It is typical that it was the trading centres of Ribe and Hedeby that produced their own coins. In Hedeby, Ohthere could see and use early Nordic coins such as these, which bore a depiction of two roosters on the one side and a fine ship motif on the other. Six specimens of this kind of coin are known. This specimen, which only recently came to light and is exhibited here for the first time, has the most detail in its motifs, which presumably makes it the oldest in the sequence.[2]

The majority of the coins from Hedeby were imitations of the coins minted by Charles the Great, or Charlemagne (r. 768–814 CE) in Dorestad in the Rhineland.[3] Imitations of this type were still being minted in Hedeby 150 years after Charles' death. On some of the coins from the early 9th century, the inscription on the reverse was replaced with images of ships, houses or people walking. A small group of coins includes images on both sides, such as the coin with the ship and roosters. Their affiliation to Hedeby is, however, a little less certain than in the case of the other coins.[4]

Towns constituted enclaves with different rules than the rest of society. Coinage was intended for use by merchants acting under the town's

74. Nordic coin with the image of a sailing ship, ca 2 cm in diameter. Probably minted in Hedeby. Silver, ca 825–830 CE (Photo: Werner Karrasch © Viking Ship Museum in Roskilde).

75. Several Nordic coins from the first half of the 9th century show pictures of ships (after Ellmers 1999).

trade agreements. The king supported the development of towns and most likely levied duties on trade. He was probably also responsible for the minting of coins. In the rest of society, coins were viewed as rare, exotic and exciting prestige items. Many coins were converted into pendants, which may have been attributed symbolic importance.[5]

Ship images The ship was a significant symbol during the Viking Age and countless examples exist, as depictions, ship-shaped stone-settings and in boat burials.[6] Dated to the 820s, the ship images from the Hedeby coins are among the earliest solidly dated depictions of sail-driven vessels in Scandinavia. Although the idea of minting ships on coins was inspired by the Christian parts of Europe,[7] it can be presumed that in reality, the ships they depicted were Scandinavian – Viking ships.[8]

The ship on this coin is unique in many ways. It is characterised by a hull with a high, sweeping stem and stern, both topped with animal heads. Animal-headed stems and sterns are often found in other ship depictions, but not on the Hedeby coins. Another feature is the row of dots in the upper edge of the hull, interpreted as oar holes. A mast stands centrally in the ship, supported by rigging. An unclear mark can be seen on the top of the mast, where in some other ship depictions one would see a cross or wind vane – perhaps this identified the ship as a flagship? Only the mast is represented, not the sail, placing this coin among the minority of the Hedeby coins; the majority of them also depict a sail.

Ships of this period had a single square sail: a square sailcloth hanging from a round spar – the yard – at the top of the mast. Due to the lack of archaeological finds, there is an ongoing debate as to the exact shape of the sail. However, Viking-Age images – sailing ships on coins, rune stones, pictorial stones and graffiti – depict a sail that in appearance is twice as wide as it is high.[9]

Other features are also included in Viking-Age ship depictions. Shields are often seen along the sides of ships and carved animal heads on the stem and stern, and occasionally also armed men on board. That a warship decorated so many of the Hedeby coins was a natural consequence of their importance in the political hotspots of the early Viking Age.[10] Today, the small ship depictions are an essential element in our understanding of the technology – sailing ships – that carried Ohthere through the North to Hedeby.

NETWORKS 105

76. The archaeological site of Aylah (in the foreground), looking over the modern city of Aqaba, Jordan, to the Red Sea (Photo: Kristoffer Damgaard).

KRISTOFFER DAMGAARD

Aylah, "Palestine's harbour on the China Sea"

"Palestine's harbour on the China Sea" was how the Arabic geographer, al-Muqaddasi, described the town of Aylah, when he visited it in the 10th century.[1] Al-Muqaddasi's descriptions show just how far-reaching an Islamic harbour town's mercantile connections could be in the Middle Ages, and the very fact that the Red Sea is denoted as the "China Sea" reflects the enormous importance of these connections during the period. Almost 20 years of excavation have underlined the town's significance in terms of Middle Eastern trade networks.[2] Aylah, situated in the modern-day Jordanian port of Aqaba, constitutes one of the most important archaeological sources in terms of understanding the development of urban environments and trade networks in the Islamic world.

As in the North, this was a time marked by the broadening of geographical horizons. In the wake of the expansion of Islam, many new towns were established. This was especially prevalent in areas of strategic importance, exemplified by Aylah. The Red Sea was an important region with a wide range of valuable and sought-after goods, such as gold, incense and African slaves. Harbour towns along the Red Sea were connected to land-based trade networks that stretched far into Africa and the Arabic lands, bringing important wares to the coastal trad-

77. Gold *dinars*, ca 2 cm in diameter, minted in Sijilmasa, Morocco, and found in a cache by D. Whitcomb at Aylah (Photo: Henrik Brahe, Aylah Archaeological Project).

106 NETWORKS

78. A Fatimid-period glass weight with an illegible inscription, ca 2 cm in diameter. Found in Aylah with other glass weights and four fine bronze bowls from a scale – presumably for weighing precious commodities such as spices or gold dust (Photo: Henrik Brahe, Aylah Archaeological Project).

ing centres. However, the Red Sea was also a maritime corridor that connected the cultures around the Mediterranean with those around the Indian Ocean, making Aylah an important centre for international trade and the "Maritime Silk Road".[3]

From an administrative perspective, Aylah was of no great importance and neither was it a particularly large town. However, its ideal location made Aylah an important Arab emporium and one of the points where the maritime network ended, to be replaced by caravans. The archaeological finds include amphorae, glazed ceramics from Egypt, Iraq and Persia, soapstone vessels from the Arabian Peninsula and even stoneware and porcelain from China.[4] Ceramicists in the early Islamic world made great technological advances in terms of glazing techniques and the beautiful glazed ceramics quickly became widely-used domestic items. Vessels of this type complied with the Koran's rule that gold and silver were amongst the delights of paradise, reserved for the righteous (43:71). They were decorated with abstract and figurative motifs, which were either painted on during firing or carved into the underglaze. A special type was the so-called lustre glaze, where metal oxides in the glaze resulted a finish resembling precious metals. The technique was originally developed in Iraq/Iran, however by around the year 1000, similar vessels were being produced from Central Asia to Tunisia. These were highly coveted luxury goods that were traded all over the Islamic world. These types of serving dishes were sometimes decorated with depictions of banquets and drinking scenes, reflecting the pomp and ceremony with which the Muslim elite surrounded themselves.

The archaeological site was first discovered in 1985, after which an American project commenced 10 years of excavations. Since 2010, the archaeological investigation of this Arab emporium has been continued by a Danish-lead project.[5] This project focuses on the town's southwestern quadrant: the mercantile area with market places, workshops, warehouses, administration buildings and more. Although Aylah was planned in accordance with the principles of antiquity (a square town with straight main streets terminating at the town gates), the town's character changed over time as its residents aadjusted the urban space to suit their changing needs. The large main streets gradually became residential areas, market places and urban institutions. New buildings were erected, town gates blocked up and new entrances broken through the town walls. The biggest change however, was the increasing focus on trade infrastructure. Market places and trading houses were established and the town wall's symbolic towers were transformed into either businesses or refuse dumps. In addition to its importance as a trading centre, Aylah was also the culmination of the pilgrim road over Sinai (Darb al-Hajj) and an important stopping point for Muslim pilgrims from North Africa and Spain – a cosmopolitan town, filled with merchants, sailors, pilgrims, craftsmen and scholars.

79. A large coarse-grained ca 60 cm-high celadon storage jar, called Dusun ware, from eastern China, 9th–11th centuries (Photo: Donald Whitcomb).

NETWORKS 107

SORNA KHAKZAD &
ATHENA TRAKADAS

The world in a grain of sand: Siraf

80. A lustreware bowl with animal motif from southern Iraq, ca 9th or 10th century, ca 20 cm in diameter. This type of ceramic was found amongst the other imports in Siraf (The David Collection, Copenhagen, Denmark. Inv. no. Isl 205).

81. A Changsha bowl from southern China, found in Siraf. Similar types were found on the Belitung shipwreck in Indonesia. Stoneware, ca 14 cm in diameter, mid 8th to early 10th century (© Trustees of the British Museum).

When Abhara voyaged to China from his adopted home port of Siraf in the 9th century, he sailed from a city at the height of its prosperity, brought about by its role in trade networks.

Siraf lay on the east coast of the Persian Gulf, on the edge of a shallow bay partially occupied today by the fishing village of Bandar-e-Taheri, Iran. The city stretched along a narrow and dry coastal strip, backed by the high Zagros Mountains foothills. Goods brought here by large cargo ships on the "Maritime Silk Road" routes were traded inland via caravan through one of the few mountain passes to Shiraz, itself a thriving market of the Abbasid Caliphate that traded locally-manufactured and imported wares.[1] Siraf was also connected to other Gulf ports that interacted in local re-distribution networks: Basra and Uballah to the north and Sohar to the south.[2] But its prosperity derived mainly from its role in direct long-distance trade that began in the mid 8th century. This trade soon increased: ca 844–48 CE, Ibn Khurradādhbih notes that Jewish merchants of the city traded with both the Mediterranean and India.[3] In 851, Sulayman the Merchant (as recounted by Abu Zayd al-Sirafi) tells that 'Chinese vessels' began calling directly at Siraf, whilst Sirafi merchants trans-shipped these goods to southern Arabia and East Africa.[4]

Trade items, well-documented archaeologically and by the 9th- and 10th-century writers al-Faqih, Abu Zayd, al-Isfahani and Buzurg Ibn Shahriyar, included woven fabrics and cotton,

82. West meets East. The obverse of a Byzantine *solidus* of Constans II, minted in Constantinople between 651–659 CE. An example struck from the same die was found in Siraf. Gold, 2.2 cm in diameter (© Trustees of the British Museum).

horses, ceramics, *dibbs* (date syrup), frankincense and pearls from the Persian Gulf; antimony for cosmetics and medicine, rugs, precious stones from Syria and Egypt; slaves, ivory, teak, ambergris, tortoise shell, and gold from East Africa; pepper, camphor, muslin and spices from India; and silk and porcelain from China.[5]

The profits of trade created wealthy Sirafi merchants. Writers of the 9th and 10th centuries such as al-Muqaddasi, al-Tabari, Yakut, Ibn al-Balkhi, and al-Istakhrī describe Siraf's elegant multi-storied houses that were constructed with palm and teak wood imported from the land of the Zanj (East Africa).[6] The Abbasid settlement had been built on top of an earlier small Sasanian-period site, with a large Congregational Mosque established in 803–804, with numerous houses and bazaars soon to follow – making it almost as large as Shiraz. Merchants were rumoured to spend 30,000 *dinars* (equivalent to 127 kg of gold) on a house.[7] The 10th-century geographer Ibn Hawqal tells of a merchant of the city, Ahmed b. 'Umar, who "... possessed a considerable fortune; a manager handled his business affairs; he had contacts with partners and agents far away; his warehouses were overflowing with spices, precious stones and perfumes; his vessels sailed to India and China, as well as the African coast".[8]

While Siraf's connections with the wider world served the port city well, its situation on a desert coastline meant that it suffered from a harsh and dry climate. Networks of wells, cisterns and aqueducts were built and local pottery and glass-making industries managed to exist. However, to survive, the population needed caravan routes from inland to supply their food and ships to import every-day items alongside exotic goods.

83. East meets West. A Tang Dynasty coin of Emperor Wu Tsung (840–846 CE), minted in China. A similar example was found in Siraf. Bronze, ca 2 cm in diameter. Left: obverse; right: reverse (National Museum of Denmark, The Royal Collection of Coins and Medals).

Al-Muqaddasi reports that an earthquake in 977 greatly affected Siraf.[9] Archaeological evidence has revealed that occupation continued and there was no immediate collapse, but the political situation had changed.[10] The breakdown of Abbasid and local dynastic control in the region in the mid 11th century gave rise to local khan rulers near the Strait of Hormuz, and shifts in alliances caused Sirafi merchants to settle elsewhere in the Gulf and Indian Ocean. The port cities of Sohar and Kish in the south began to control the Gulf's Indian Ocean trade. Although the Congregational Mosque of Siraf was kept in repair and the cemeteries were still used in the 12th century, the short-lived fortunes of the once-prosperous port city had by this time passed.[11]

84. During the 9th and 10th centuries, Siraf was a major Persian Gulf port from which numerous ships set sail and hopefully returned, following "Maritime Silk Road" routes. Its ruins can now be seen among the fishing village of Bandar-e-Taheri, Iran (Photo: Athena Trakadas).

85. Unguja Ukuu, the site of one of the most important East African emporia, on the shores of Menai Bay, Zanzibar (Photo: Tom Fitton).

STEPHANIE WYNNE-JONES,
ALISON CROWTHER & MARK HORTON

Zanzibar: a network society

Zanzibar is both an archipelago off the coast of central Tanzania and a name commonly used for its largest island. Before the 15th century, Zanzibar, from Arabic *al-bahr al-Zanj* ("Zanj Sea"), appears in Islamic geographies, implying a much larger section of the East African coast, where the people of the region were known to the Arabic-speaking world as the Zanj.[1] The much older name for Zanzibar island, *Unguja*, may derive from the Bantu –*ngoja* ("to wait"), referring to the collection of goods awaiting the change in monsoons.[2]

Unguja is preserved in the toponym Unguja Ukuu ("Great Unguja"). The antiquity of this place-name is demonstrated by the Arabic treatise *The Book of Curiosities of the Sciences and Marvels for the Eyes*, compiled in Egypt before ca 1050 CE.[3] A map from a 12th–13th century copy of the treatise shows the coasts of the Indian Ocean from China to East Africa. Among the key islands shown are *Qanbalu* (probably Pemba, the second-largest island in the Zanzibar archipelago) and *Unjuwa* (Unguja). The latter island "has a town called Ukuh".[4]

86. Glass beads found during recent excavations at Unguja Ukuu, ca 700–950 CE (Photo: Ian Cartwright, School of Archaeology, University of Oxford).

1 cm

87. Local and imported pottery found on Unguja Ukuu, Zanzibar. The turquoise glazed pieces come from the Persian Gulf; the piece at top right comes from India; the light brown glazed piece at the right is from southern China, ca 700–950 CE (Photo: Jason Hawkes).

Unguja Ukuu on Zanzibar island's southern coast was one of the most important East African settlements of the 7th to 10th centuries. It has been excavated only in small part, but bears an immensely rich assemblage of goods relating to both local production and trade during that period.[5] From around 800 CE stone buildings were constructed along the busy waterfront, including a probable mosque.[6] This represents early conversion to Islam in this region, no doubt reflecting the intensity of connections between Unguja Ukuu and the Islamic heartlands.

The Unguja Ukuu community farmed, fished and also produced goods for exchange, manufacturing shell beads and iron.[7] Foreign traders that visited this shore left ceramics, beads and vessels; these are only a fraction of cargoes that do not preserve well, which included date products and oils, as well as foodstuffs such as rice. Turquoise alkaline glazed wares arrived from the Persian Gulf likely carrying foodstuffs, carnelian beads arrived from India (probably Gujarat), and some glass beads arrived from Southeast Asia. These goods are evidence for trade contacts not mentioned by contemporary histories, which archaeologists are only beginning to understand. A bronze mirror found during 2011 excavations is likely from China, although this may have come via intermediaries.[8]

Yet communities of Zanzibar were not simply trading emporia. They were varied and complex societies, many of which had rich leaders.[9] The best

88. Fragment of a bronze mirror, probably Chinese, found at Unguja Ukuu, ca 700–950 CE (Photo: Ian Cartwright, School of Archaeology, University of Oxford).

89. The Mtambwe Mkuu hoard, comprising more than 2,000 coins minted by African rulers, together with a few imported gold coins, excavated at Mtambwe Mkuu, Pemba Island, Zanzibar (Photo: Mark Horton).

90. Silver coins of Ali bin al-Hasan, Sultan of Kilwa, ca 11th century. Recovered as part of the Mtambwe Mkuu hoard, Pemba Island, Zanzibar (Photo: Mark Horton).

evidence for these rulers comes from the coins that were struck on the Swahili coast from the 9th century onwards. The Mtambwe Mkuu hoard, found on Pemba island, is one of the most important hoards found in Zanzibar and contains coins minted by East African rulers in the 10th and 11th centuries alongside imported gold coins from the Fatimid and Abbasid Caliphates. Three examples of the Mtambwe silver coins were found in excavations at Unguja Ukuu, while an earlier find included around 500 gold *dinars*, probably from the early Abbasid period. On Zanzibar island, copper coins continued to be minted by local rulers, including the sultans of Tumbatu, until the 14th century. Together these coins testify to the incorporation of the Zanzibar archipelago into international systems of value, and demonstrate the importance of local rulers and settlements. The different types found in each place, locally-minted but broadly accepted, illustrate well the nature of East African sites. This conjures up a world in which each settlement was independent, yet recognised the authority of their neighbours and accepted their coinage as part of a broader exchange network in which they all participated.

JOHN MIKSIC

The Srivijaya Empire and its maritime aspects

The Empire of Srivijaya ("Glorious Victory") appeared in history in the 7th century, when a Chinese Buddhist pilgrim sailed from China to Sumatra and then to India on royal Srivijayan ships.[1] It seems at this time, the sea route through the Straits of Melaka was gradually becoming more popular than the portage route across the Siamo-Malay Peninsula. This change probably correlates with developments in seafaring technology among the Sumatrans, and the realisation among Southeast Asians that local incense and medicinal plants could be substituted for those from the Arabo-Persian world, in demand in China.[2]

Srivijaya was also a centre of trade in local luxuries such as gold, ivory, pepper, camphor, cloves, nutmeg, sandalwood, star anise, and a range of other exotic items sought by Asian elites.[3]

91. General view of the 9th-century Buddhist temple at Borobudur, central Java, Indonesia. Watercolour on paper, published by J. Honig and Zoonen, 1814 (© Trustees of the British Museum).

NETWORKS 115

Much of the Srivijayan Empire's own maritime trade was conducted by Indonesians who sailed as far as Madagascar by the 6th century.

Srivijaya ruled the Straits of Melaka for the next 350 years. Nobody could sail between the Indian Ocean and the South China Sea without coming within range of the kingdom's navy, including its tax collectors who levied duties on all passing ships. The kingdom's capital at Palembang was located exactly one sailing season's distance from India or China. A trader from the Persian Gulf could take as long as two years to get to China and back, with good weather.[4] Many preferred to trade in Sumatra, so that they could return home in half the time.

Buddhism, the main religion in Srivijaya, was very similar to that which inspired the great monument of Borobudur. The Buddhist emblems on the gold trays and Changsha bowls found on the 9th-century Belitung shipwreck and at Abhara's home port of Siraf would have been suitable for use in monasteries in Java and Sumatra, where sherds of such wares have been found by archaeologists.[5]

Historians emphasise the importance of Chinese trade in fostering Srivijaya's development, but contemporary Arab and Indian writers paid more attention to the kingdom's ports of Kedah (*Kalah*) and Barus. Much Arabic literature on Southeast Asia written during the 9th and 10th centuries consists of sailors' tales such as Buzurg Ibn Shahriyar's *The Marvels of the Wonders of India*, and was derived from people who had actually been there, with much embellishment. Buzurg echoes Indian literature in calling Southeast Asia the "Land of Gold," and *Kalah* appears in the voyages of Sindbad in the *Arabian Nights*.[6]

Some scholars believe that political power in Srivijaya was diffused among several locations. Palembang probably monopolised the China trade, whereas Barus, on Sumatra's northwest coast, referred to in Chinese as Srivijaya's "second capital", is much richer in artefacts from the Persian Gulf.[7]

Arab sources often mention *Kalah*, the Malaysian state of Kedah at the northeast entrance to the Straits of Melaka, and say it was under the authority of the maharaja of *Zabag*, a vague Arabic term sometimes used for south Sumatra and west Java, and sometimes specifically Srivijaya.[8]

In 758 CE the Arabo-Persian community, who had been trading directly in China since the early 8th century, sacked the southern port of Guangzhou, and moved their operations to *Kalah* for the next 40 years.[9] In 878 Guangzhou was pillaged by Chinese rebels, and foreigners, including many ships from Oman, again moved to *Kalah*.[10] Archaeological sites of ports in this area contain artefacts from both west Asia and China.[11]

Later, Arab merchants took passage to Guangzhou on a ship from *Kulo* (probably Kedah) in 1012.[12] On several occasions Srivijayan embassies used their access to Arab goods to impress the Chinese government.[13] Tribute from Srivijaya in 1017 or 1018 contained a huge quantity of Arab commodities, as well as Indonesian produce.

In 1025 Srivijaya suffered a devastating raid from south India. Kedah and Barus seem to have come under direct Indian control for the next century, while the main port in southeast Sumatra moved to the Kingdom of Malayu. Sumatra, however, remained an important intermediary between China and west Asia, shown by such deeds as the gift of sent 189 pieces of glassware by Malayu to the Song royal court in 1178.[14] Srivijaya's successors thus continued to play the role of intermediary between China and the Arabo-Persian region until at least the 13th century.

92. An idealised royal court scene, as depicted at the 9th-century Borobudur temple, central Java, Indonesia (Tropenmuseum, Amsterdam. Object number 10015843).

93. A Buddha head that once decorated the temple at Borobudur. Volcanic stone, ca 45 cm high, dated to the 9th century (© Trustees of the British Museum).

NETWORKS 117

JUN KIMURA

Seafaring in the Far East

Throughout history, shipping and maritime trade have been critical to the development of human societies. In Southeast Asia, powerful maritime kingdoms such as the Srivijaya Empire (7th–13th centuries), in what is now present-day Indonesia, were notable for maintaining their rule over several centuries.[1] The power and longevity of these kingdoms were due to the dominant positions they held within the maritime trading system, in a region which encompasses numerous archipelagos and large gulfs. As seaborne goods are still being discovered at many inshore archaeological sites, the trading networks must have reached deep into riverine systems. Sites are typically located in river deltas or on islets, and include ruins of port cities. These sites are of major importance for understanding the maritime trade of the region's rich and diverse goods, including spices, silks, beads, ceramics, metal ingots and religious items.[2] Recent research clarifies the extent to which far-flung settlements and trading activities many centuries ago were connected by sea routes and sophisticated ships.

But what types of ships played a role in these extensive maritime networks of Southeast Asia? During the 9th century, when Abhara sailed from the Persian Gulf to China, many indigenous ships sailed in Southeast Asian waters. Clues about their appearance can still be found. Images of seaworthy ships from this period are depicted in carvings on the Borobudur temple,

94. One of the ships depicted on the 9th-century Buddhist temple at Borobudur, central Java, Indonesia. Ships in Southeast Asia at this time might have appeared very similar, with a stabilising outrigger and tri-pod masts (Tropenmuseum, Amsterdam. Object number 20025669).

a Buddhist monument built in central Java in the early 9th century. One of these carvings has provoked much discussion about the representative features of ships used by Southeast Asian seafarers. The realistic depiction of the hull and outriggers reveals a ship capable of conducting long ocean voyages. Other details of the relief include unique features endemic to ships from the region. The hull shows a stem-post projecting from the bow, and the ship has quarter rudders on its stern, and tri-pod masts. A stabilising outrigger is another distinctive feature of early Southeast Asian seagoing ships.

But evidence also exists from archaeological finds. One of the most important is the ancient boats at Butuan in Mindanao, in the present-day Philippines.[3] Significantly, ship timbers showing similar construction methods to those used on the Butuan boats have been discovered in Malaysia, Thailand, and Indonesia.[4] Some of these historical remains have been dated to the first half of the first millennia – indicating the early maturity of shipbuilding across a region in which such traditions have remained an important aspect of societies and cultures to the present day. The structures of these early seaworthy ships reveal an important innovation: reinforcement of the transverse structure using frames attached to protrusions on the inner surface of the hull planks (called lugs) by vegetable fibres. This innovation, along with a construction technique that relies on edged-joining the planks with a combination of stitching and wooden dowels, characterise the Southeast Asian boatbuilding tradition and identify early ships of the region.[5]

Remains of early medieval vessels bearing the hallmarks of local shipbuilding techniques are being found in increasing numbers, as more Southeast Asian countries explore their maritime archaeology. In Thailand, ship timbers were recovered from a channel in Koh Kwang Village (Muang District, Chanthaburi Province) and boat remains have been found in a river near Kok Yang temple in Kantang, Tran Province. In Brunei, ship timbers have been found near the Brunei River.[6] These discoveries illustrate similarities in a construction method, and point to indigenous origin. One remarkable recent discovery, in 2008, was of a well-preserved ship at Punjulharjo Village (Central Java Province, Indonesia) – around 1 km inland from the present-day coast. The ship's hull measured 15 × 5 m, and its surface featuring aligned lugs (*tambuku*) allowing 12 frames to be attached. This ship was radiocarbon-dated to 660–780 CE.[7]

95. The 'Butuan Boat 1' find at the Balangay Shirine in Butuan City, the Philippines. Dated to 320 CE (Photo: L.S.P. Lacsina).

NETWORKS 119

96. The Punjulharjo ship found in central Java, Indonesia. Dated to the 7th or 8th century (Photo: P.-Y. Manguin).

Many other shipwrecks in Indonesian waters also show evidence of local Southeast Asian origin, including the Intan, Cirebon, and Karawang shipwrecks, which all date from around the 10th century. As countries throughout the region explore rich underwater sites, reports are trickling in about similar discoveries, including off the coast of Sabah in Borneo, near Gunjangan Island in Sulu Province in the Philippines, and near Cu Lao Cham Island off the central Vietnam coast.[8] To date, ship remains discovered at both underwater and land sites that include features consistent with Southeast Asian shipbuilding traditions spread over six countries in the region. These findings support the hypothesis that key boatbuilding innovations were disseminated widely around the coasts here, and it is predicted that many similar wrecks remain to be discovered.

Importantly, the waters off mainland and archipelagic Southeast Asia were both intra- and inter-regional sea-lanes, where local ships co-existed with other types of vessels from more distant regions. In particular, merchants from the Indian Ocean regions are known to have appeared early in Southeast Asian maritime history. One report of seafaring by Indian merchants in the 5th century is illustrated in the pilgrimage records of a Chinese monk, Faxien, journeying from Sri Lanka to China via Java. The ship he sailed in, a Brahmin Indian ship, is considered likely to be identical to a ship depicted among the famous cave paintings in the Ajanta Caves, India, dating to the 7th century.[9] Indian seafarers would not have been the only distant travellers encountered by Southeast Asian vessels: historical texts from China's Tang Dynasty (619–907) include records of ships of many different origins, including Sri Lanka, Persia, and the Arabian Peninsula. A major destination for these vessels at the time was Guangzhou in southern China, the end of the "Maritime Silk Road". These journeys were typically extensive. A round-trip, including time for local trading, port stop-overs for shipments, and transfers between ships, could take up to two years.[10]

Archaeological explorations of early shipwreck sites are providing a better understanding of the historical dynamics of seafaring in the Far East during the early medieval period, when Southeast Asian seafarers exerted a strong regional presence using local seaworthy ships, and mingled with sailors and merchants from the Indian Ocean world and beyond. Given the growing focus on maritime archaeology among Southeast Asian countries, further important discoveries will no doubt emerge in the future.

SØREN M. SINDBÆK

Suzhou, China, and the Maritime Silk Road

Foreign sailors were not an uncommon sight in Chinese port cities during the medieval period. Each year crowds of merchants arrived in Guangzhou on the southern coast or in Ningbo, Hangzhou and Yangzhou on the east coast. Contemporary sources even allege that thousands of Persians and Arab resided in these cities in the 8th and 9th centuries.[1] But this was a comparatively new situation. The numbers of sea-borne travellers and a resident merchant diaspora had grown in tandem with one of the most externally-oriented epochs of Chinese history, the Tang Dynasty (619–907 CE). The coastal regions were effectively integrated into central imperial policy since the construction of the Grand Canal in the early 7th century, allowing for river transport from the port of Hangzhou to the capital of Chang'an in central China and into the Hebei province to the north. But the major impact of sea trade in China developed in the second half of the 8th century, when maritime networks also grew in the western hemisphere. The effect can be seen in the measures implemented by the imperial government to harness and protect it: a maritime trade commissioner was appointed for the first time in 763, and foreign merchants were granted imperial protection in 829.[2]

The influence of maritime trade was not only felt in the ports. Suzhou in the Jiangsu province, near Shanghai, was a major regional centre striding the Grand Canal. It was a city of canals and bridges and of famous Buddhist temples – a religion brought to China by travellers – that attracted pilgrims. Moreover, it was a hub for the manufacture of silk, one of China's chief export commodities. For the citizens of Suzhou, the maritime expansion could be seen in the busy run of cargo boats on the Canal, the foreign visitors in the temples, and the thriving business of the silk works.

97. Chinese barges preparing to pass under a bridge in Suzhou. Watercolour by William Alexander, ca 1796 (© Trustees of the British Museum).

Refined and beautiful, and eminently portable, silk textiles were carried for centuries over land from China throughout Asia and into the Middle East and Europe along the network of caravan routes known collectively as the Silk Road. For long a closely guarded industrial secret, the art of cultivating and manufacturing silk had, by the time of the Tang emperors, also reached Persia and the Mediterranean world; yet silk remained a defining Chinese industry. The sea offered new routes for its export, a "Maritime Silk Road". But the rise of sea travel also opened the world to a different range of artisan products – items too heavy or too bulky to transport easily and economically over extended land routes. This opportunity spurred an original product that became a trademark of China for another millennium: porcelain.[3]

The development of Chinese ceramics into refined luxury products was encouraged by another foreign encounter. Buddhist monks and pilgrims increasingly travelled between India and China in the Tang period, and introduced to China the custom of drinking tea. This fashion created a demand for heat resistant wares that would complement élite tables set with precious metal plates and ewers. While the early Tang period is renowned for the production of colourful lead-glazed pottery figurines used to furnish elaborate burials, the 8th century saw the proliferation of fine glazed table wares.

98. White porcelain dish. Diameter 14 cm, Tang Dynasty, 619–907 CE. From excavations at the northern city wall in Xiang Gate, Suzhou (Suzhou Museum, China).

99. Celadon lamp in the shape of a lotus. Height 11.3 cm, Five Dynasties Period, 907–960 CE. From excavations to the south of Tiger Hill, Suzhou (Suzhou Museum, China).

White porcelain was the hallmark of kilns in northern China. Earlier, Chinese potters had experimented with white wares and glazed ceramics, but during the Tang period the full development of the product was realised, becoming synonymous in many languages with the country itself: China, or porcelain. Thinly potted from white kaolin clay, fired at very high temperatures and covered with a sparkling clear glaze, it was for centuries a model of elegance and technical accomplishment. Vessels produced for use in China were almost invariably finished in pure white glaze, the colour of silver, but wares decorated with patterns of blue or green glazing were produced specifically for export to markets in South East Asia and in the Middle East. The fact that tastes in overseas societies influenced artisan production to create an export industry is vivid testimony to the impact of sea routes.[4]

Potters in southern China specialised in a product of equal distinction. Green glazes complement the yellow-firing clays of the region to produce a texture reminiscent of polished jade: celadon. The best celadon wares were produced in the Yue kilns, in the region neighbouring Suzhou. The Tang poet Lu Yu (ca 730–ca 804), in *The Classic of Tea*, praises Yue wares for the subtle way in which their glaze enhances the colour of tea.[5] Like white porcelain, celadon ware was soon exported along the sea lanes of Asia.[6] Sherds are found in archaeological sites in Indonesia, India and Sri Lanka, in East African emporia, and throughout the Middle East. Not without a reason, the "Maritime Silk Road" is also sometimes dubbed "The Ceramic Road".[7]

In return for manufactured goods, precious metals were important commodities imported to China, but occasionally fine metalwork was also exported. Twenty-nine cast bronze mirrors were found in a single cargo in the 9th century shipwreck found off Belitung, Indonesia,[8] and fragments of similar mirrors are occasionally found in East African emporia. They carry a millennia-old tradition of Chinese craftsmanship into foreign lands, along with elaborate images of Chinese cosmology. But the decoration of Tang period mirrors also reflects China's encounter with the world: floral ornaments and naturalistic scenes inspired by Hellenistic and Persian art, and scenes and symbols of Buddhist legends. These elements blend and resonate in the designs, as in the poetry of the Tang period. A lone traveller to Suzhou's famous Hanshan (literally 'Cold Mountain') temple, evoked by the poet Zhang Ji (ca 715–779), is pictured in a scene which would have made a fitting theme for the dim reflection of a bronze mirror:

"While I watch the moon go down, a crow caws through the frost; Under the shadows of maple-trees a fisherman moves with his torch; And I hear, from beyond Suzhou, from the temple on Cold Mountain, ringing for me, here in my boat, the midnight bell."
– Zhang Ji, *A Night Mooring by Maple Bridge in Suzhou*[9]

100. Bronze mirror in the shape of an eight-petal water-chestnut flower, decorated with fabulous animals. Copper alloy, 15.2 cm in diameter, Tang Dynasty, 619–907 CE. From excavations at Shangtang River (Suzhou Museum, China).

NETWORKS 123

SØREN M. SINDBÆK &
ATHENA TRAKADAS

The journey of ideas

As sailors explored new routes and cargos changed hands, ideas and beliefs also travelled by sea. In this way the map of world religions was redrawn.

The message of the prophet Mohammed was transferred beyond the borders of the Islamic world by Muslim merchants who practised their religion when they sailed or travelled abroad. Mosques emerged along the coast of East Africa and in India and Sri Lanka, and Islam gained ground as far north as the Volga.[1] The words of Islam were also disseminated in copies of Korans. A fragment of a fine manuscript, made in what is now southern Iraq in the 9th or 10th centuries, shows what a Muslim would have seen and heard read in the mosque. The script is typical of the *mashq* calligraphic style, one of the earliest Arabic scripts, and known to have been practised in Kufa, Basra and Baghdad at this time.[2] The elongated horizontal lines were written in black and red ink on parchment – a writing surface made using a technique that originated centuries earlier in the eastern Mediterranean.

But Islam was not the first religion to travel via ship through the Indian Ocean world. On the islands of Java and Sumatra, Indian and Chinese pilgrims made the sea kingdom of Srivijaya a centre for Buddhist and Hindu learning.[3] Buddhism and Hinduism had been spreading though pilgrimages and contacts with merchants on the trade routes from Southeast Asia to China. This had begun with the conversion of the Indian emperor Asoka in the 3rd century BCE.[4] In the 8th and 9th centuries, as rulers in Java began to construct mighty stone temples and increasing numbers of pilgrims visited the island, imported bronze figures began to decorate shrines.[5] One of these was a small bronze figure of Tara made in west Bengal in the 9th century, but found in Java. The overall style of the figure – its head-dress, shape and background – indicates an Indian origin, which tended to be less ornate than contemporary Southeast Asian

101. Two pages from a Koran from Kufa, Basra or Baghdad, Iraq. Passage from Sura 2, vers. 249–254, also referred to as *al-Baqara*, or 'the cow'. Parchment, ca 800–1000 CE (The David Collection, Copenhagen, Denmark. Inv. no. 31/1974).

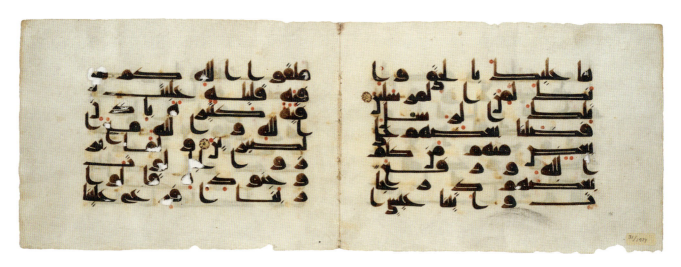

102. Tara figure made in west Bengal. Found on Java, Indonesia. Bronze, 13 cm high, ca 800 CE (© Trustees of the British Museum).

covered in complex patterns derived from Celtic art, and probably copied from Irish metal ornaments or from a manuscript. Also striking are two prominent wheel crosses. An unintentional use of this religious symbol is difficult to reconcile with the cross-cultural interactions exemplified in the imported objects of this grave. How this symbolism was understood and interpreted is a different matter. Along with Christian symbolism the brooch also pays homage to a traditional pagan image: two bosses mark the eyes of a crouched beast, while four similar bosses mark the joints of its front and hind legs. The Christian symbolism in the Svennevig brooch had literally been carried into a foreign country.

103. Oval brooch from a woman's grave at Svennevig near Grimstad, Norway. Copper alloy, 8.2 cm long, ca 800 CE (Photo: Adnan Icagic, Museum of Cultural History, University of Oslo).

examples. The Tara figure is a representation of a Hindu mother goddess, of generous compassion, but she was also venerated by Buddhists as a Bodhisattva – someone who has attained an enlightened mind and was a symbol of virtue. Thus Buddhism and Hinduism often travelled together, reaching new lands as spiritual companions.

In Scandinavia, Christian churches were established by Frankish missionaries arriving between ca 825–850 in three emporia: Ribe, Hedeby and Birka. They may have served foreign merchants as much as local converts, yet finds show that some natives received Christianity.[6] A brooch from Svennevig near Grimstad in southern Norway, almost certainly cast in Scandinavia, shows the transfer of religious ideals.[7] The brooch (one of a pair) was discovered in a woman's burial in a mound together with other objects, including a reworked ornament and a jet bead from the British Isles – rare items suggesting a cosmopolitan milieu. The surface is

NETWORKS 125

Notes

P. 3
Foreword

1. The conference, "Maritime Networks and Urbanism in the Early Medieval World", was held from the 11th–12th April 2013 at the Viking Ship Museum. The conference abstracts have been published at http://projekter.au.dk/entrepot/.

PP. 8–11
The World in the Viking Age
SØREN M. SINDBÆK

1. The Belitung wreck provides an important new source on early medieval ships in the Indian Ocean, and its cargo is by far the most extensive collection of the types of goods that traders in this region brought back from their voyages to Tang-period China. However, the finds from the wreck were recovered by a for-profit salvage operation, and the Viking Ship Museum, in line with UNESCO conventions, will not condone such activities by displaying the operation's finds to the public.
2. Sharma 1987; Horden & Purcell 2000; Wickham 2005.
3. Hourani 1995.
4. Wang 2003.
5. McCormick 2001.
6. Chaudhuri 1985: 102; Sindbæk 2007; Wynne-Jones 2007; Hodges 2012a; Miksic 2013.

PP. 14–20
Ohthere's voyages
JANET BATELY

1. For Wulfstan's voyage see Bately 1980: 16.21–18.2; Bately 2009.
2. Stevenson 1904: §76.
3. Keynes & Lapidge 1983; Zangemeister 1882.
4. Bately 1980: 12.24–13.28; Bately 2007: 22–26. For detailed identification of people and places, see Bately 2007: 51–58.
5. Bately 1980: 13.29–16.20; Bately 2007: 32–34, 44–47.
6. Or five? See Bately 2007: 57–58.
7. Bately 2007: 35–39.
8. Bately 1980: 188–189, 191; Bately 2007: 57–58; Storli 2007: 90–94.
9. Bately 1980: 191–192.
10. See Christensen 2007.
11. Storli 2007: 85–87, 97–98, and, for a different scenario, Sawyer 2007: 136–139.
12. Scudder & Oskarsdottir 2002: Chs 10 and 16.
13. See, e.g., Storli 2007: 87–88.
14. Scudder & Oskarsdottir 2002: Chs 8, 9, 10, 17; Storli 2007: 95–97.
15. See Brink 2007; Englert 2007; Makarov 2007; Skre 2007a.
16. So Paulus Diaconus, in Foulke & Peters 2003: I.6.
17. For *healh* see Gelling & Cole 2000: 123–133.
18. Skre 2007a: 150–156; Bately 2007: 37–38, 55–56; Müller-Wille 2007: 157–165.
19. Scudder & Oskarsdottir 2002: Ch. 17.
20. Bately 1986: annal for 896.

PP. 21–25
The making of the Viking Age
SØREN M. SINDBÆK

1. Bately & Englert 2007; see also Bately, this volume, pp. 14–20.
2. Munch et al. 2003.
3. Sjøvold 1974.
4. Roesdahl 2003; Barrett et al. 2011.
5. Roesdahl 1992.
6. E.g., Goodacre et al. 2005; Wallace 2011; Kershaw 2013.
7. Skre 2011.
8. Ambrosiani & Clarke 1995; Callmer 2007; Skre 2007b; Skre 2008; Hodges 2012a.
9. Pestell & Ulmschneider 2003.
10. Steuer 2009.
11. Callmer 1995.
12. Barrett et al. 2011; Becker & Grupe 2012.
13. Callmer 2002; Sindbæk 2007.
14. Holm et al. 2005.
15. Olsen 2003.
16. Barrett 2008.
17. Sindbæk 2011.

PP. 26–29
Scandinavian ships and seafaring
ANTON ENGLERT

1. Rieck 1998.
2. Varenius 1992: 62–68, 80–85, figs 17–22, figs 24–27; Imer 2004: 104, Table 17; Christensen 1998: 206–213; Bonde & Stylegar 2009.
3. Haywood 1991: 72; Crumlin-Pedersen 2010: 98.
4. Christensen 2007; see Englert, this volume, pp. 30–31.
5. *Konungs Skuggsjá* in Jónsson 1926: 60–63.
6. Makarov 2007.
7. Binns 1961; Englert 2007: 125–127.
8. Englert 2007: 119–125.
9. See Bately, this volume, pp. 14–20.
10. Müller-Wille 2009: 361–362.

PP. 30–31
Opening up the Northern Seas: the Gokstad ship
ANTON ENGLERT

1. Bonde 1994: 148.
2. Nicolaysen 1882.
3. Christensen 2007.
4. Bonde 1994: 148.
5. See Kalmring, this volume, pp. 102–103.
6. Dammann 1996.
7. Andersen 1895.
8. Christensen 2007.
9. Crumlin-Pedersen 1999.

PP. 32–33
The loom and the sail
SARAH CROIX

1. See Englert, this volume, pp. 26–29.
2. Andersen 1995; Andersen & Nørgård 2009.
3. Andersson 2003.
4. Roesdahl et al. 2014.

PP. 34–35
The Low Countries and the Northern Seas
DRIES TYS

1. Hodges 2012a.
2. Van Es & Verwers 1980.
3. Bracker et al. 1999: 218.
4. Sindbæk 2007; Skre 2008.
5. Loveluck & Tys 2006; Thomas 2012.
6. McCormick 2001; see Horsnæs, this volume, p. 65.

PP. 36–37
Arctic resources and urban networks
STEVEN P. ASHBY & ASHLEY COUTU

1. See Bately, this volume, pp. 14–20.
2. Ashby 2009; Ashby 2011.
3. Feveile 2006.
4. Von Holstein et al. 2014; Ashby et al. in preparation.
5. Roesdahl 2003.

PP. 40–45
Abhara's voyages
DIONISIUS A. AGIUS

1. The author is thankful for the support of King Abdulaziz University, Jeddah, Saudi Arabia.
2. Shafiq 2013: 56.
3. Translation Freeman-Grenville 1981: 49–52, with a few amendments by the present author.
4. Sauvaget 1948; Renaudot 1733; Dāghir 1983; De Goeje 1906.
5. Galland 1704–1717.
6. Gerhardt 1963: 239; Shafiq 2013: 32.
7. Van der Lith & Devic 1883–1886: 2, 4–5, 7, 12–14, 16–17, 19, 36, 62, 64, 98, 105, 137, 141–142, 148, 152, 165; De Goeje 1927: 138; De Goeje 1906: 18; Dāghir 1983, I: 123.
8. See Wynne-Jones, this volume, p. 50–53.
9. Dāghir 1983, I: 176; Hirth & Rockhill 1911: 33; see also Agius 2008: 77; Shafiq 2013: 64–65; see Khakzad & Trakadas, this volume, pp. 108–110.
10. Agius 2008: 56, 75–80, 101, 142, 145, 180, 238–239, 271.
11. Irwin 1994: 71.
12. Hall 2008: 49.
13. Elders 2001: 47–57.
14. See Vosmer, this volume, pp. 58–61.

pp. 46–49
The Abbasid Indian Ocean trade
TIMOTHY POWER

1. See Agius, this volume, pp. 40–45.
2. Chaudhuri 1985: 47–48.
3. Hodges & Whitehouse 1983: 147.
4. Hourani 1995: 63.
5. Adams 1965: 69–83; Adams 1981: 200–214.
6. Kennedy 2004.
7. Quoted by Hourani 1995: 64.
8. Le Strange 1966: 44–48.
9. Routes and times given in the *Akhbār al-Sīn w-al-Hind* ('News of China and India'), authorship unknown, but commented upon in the early 10th century by Abu Zayd al-Sirafi; see Hourani 1995: 69–74.
10. Hourani 1995: 74–75; Gernet 1982: 287–289.
11. Chaudhuri 1985: 47–49.
12. Lunde & Stone 2007: 104.
13. Lunde & Stone 2007: 113; see Sindbæk, this volume, pp. 121–123.
14. Insoll 2003: 169; see Wynne-Jones, this volume, pp. 50–53 for these wares in East Africa.
15. Rogers 1991.
16. Lunde & Stone 2007: 78.
17. Gernet 1996: 292; Hourani 1995: 76.
18. Hitti 1970: 344–345; Sheriff 2010: 158; see Khakzad & Trakadas, this volume, pp. 108–110.
19. Krahl *et al.* 2010; see Vosmer, this volume, pp. 58–61.
20. Northedge & Kennet 1994.
21. Hourani 1995: 77–78; Sheriff 2010: 176–177.
22. Hodges & Whitehouse 1983: 156–157.
23. Sheriff 2010: 158; Power 2012: 212–216.
24. Quoted by Sheriff 2010: 158; see Khakzad & Trakadas, this volume, pp. 108–110.

pp. 50–53
Africa's emporia
STEPHANIE WYNNE-JONES

1. So writes the Arab geographer al-Mas'udi, who travelled to Pemba Island in 915–916; Barbier de Meynard & de Courteille 1864: 6.
2. Kusimba 1999.
3. Fleisher & LaViolette 2013; Horton 1996; Juma 2004.
4. See Agius, this volume, pp. 40–45.
5. Chittick 1984.
6. Horton 1996.
7. Wright 1993.
8. Fleisher & Wynne-Jones 2011.
9. LaViolette & Fleisher 2009.
10. See also Power, this volume, pp. 46–49.
11. See also Wynne-Jones *et al.*, this volume, pp. 111–114.
12. Kusimba 1996.
13. Sinclair 1995.
14. LaViolette 2008; Wynne-Jones 2007.

pp. 54–57
Ships of the Indian Ocean
JEREMY GREEN & ATHENA TRAKADAS

1. Boussac & Salles 1995.
2. Deloche 1980; Reade 1996; Pearson 2003.
3. Hourani 1995; Parkin & Barnes 2002; Chaudhuri 1985.
4. For example, see Parkin & Barnes 2002; Ray & Salles 1996; Chaudhuri 1985.
5. Parkin & Barnes 2002.
6. Vosmer 2010; see, in this volume, Power, p. 46–49 and Vosmer, pp. 58–61.
7. Freeman-Grenville 1981: 49–52; Galland 1704–1717.
8. See Agius, this volume, pp. 40–45.
9. For example, De Goeje 1892: 360; Barbier de Meynard & de Courteille 1861: 87; Koran, Surat Qamar 54:13; see also Hourani 1995: 89–96; Agius 2005: 161–165.
10. Procopius, *Persian Wars* I.19, ll.23–26; Yule 1914: 66–67.
11. Vosmer 2010: 122.
12. See Vosmer, this volume, pp. 58–61.
13. Discussion presented in Hourani 1995: 92–97.
14. Pearson 2003.
15. Latham 1958: 53.
16. *Maqāmāt al-Hariri*, Bibliothèque nationale de France, manuscrit Arabe 5847, maqama 39; Hourani 1995: 93.
17. Agius 2008: 158–160; Vosmer 2010: 122.
18. For example, Al-Tanukhi 1955: 338; De Goeje 1892: 390.
19. Agius 2008: 268–273.
20. *Maqāmāt al-Hariri*, St. Petersburg Branch of the Institute of Oriental Studies, manuscript C-23, maqama 39.
21. Whitehouse 1970: 14–15, pl. XIIf; Vosmer 1999.
22. Manguin 1993a: 263–264; see also Kimura, this volume, pp. 118–120.
23. Broadhurst 1952: 69–70.
24. Agius 2008: 208–210; Yule 1914: 67.
25. A lateen is possibly alluded to by the 10th-century geographer al-Muqaddasi as the *muthallatha* ("triangle"), used on vessels in Mesopotamia, see Agius 2008: 212.
26. Hourani 1995; Chaudhuri 1985.

pp. 58–61
The Belitung shipwreck and *Jewel of Muscat*
TOM VOSMER

1. Latham 1958: 58.
2. Guy 2001–2002: 17.
3. See Power, this volume, pp. 46–49.
4. See Green & Trakadas, this volume, pp. 54–57.
5. Lopo Homem's *Atlas of 1519*, Biblioteque National, Paris.
6. Garlake & Garlake 1964: 201.
7. Mott 1997: 123.

pp. 62–63
Maritime rhythms of the monsoon
JULIAN WHITEWRIGHT

1. Tibbetts 1971: 360.
2. Heikell 1999: 29–32.
3. Whitewright 2011.
4. Casson 1989.
5. Tibbetts 1971.

p. 64
India in Africa
JASON HAWKES & STEPHANIE WYNNE-JONES

1. Juma 2004; Horton 1996.
2. Fleisher & Wynne-Jones 2011.
3. Francis 2002.
4. Insoll *et al.* 2004; Insoll & Bahn 2001.
5. Wood 2011.
6. Ghosh 1990.

p. 65
Changing hands: the Skovsholm *dirham* hoard
HELLE HORSNÆS

1. Petterson 2008.
2. Kovalev & Kaelin 2007.
3. Losiński 1988; Rispling 2007.
4. Laursen 2013; Horsnæs & Ingvardson *forthcoming*.
5. Eshragh 2010.

pp. 68–73
Theodosios' voyages
JONATHAN SHEPARD

1. Lilie *et al.* 1998-2002: #7874.
2. Auzépy 2008: 251–291.
3. Bekker 1838: 88–89.
4. Kocabaş 2008: 102, 164, 168–172; Kızıltan 2013; see Kocabaş, this volume, pp. 78–81.
5. See Gelichi, this volume, pp. 74–77.
6. Tsougarakis 1988: 37–46.
7. Franklin & Shepard 1996: 31.
8. Manzano Moreno 1998: 220–226; Signes Codoñer 2004: 199–201, 204-205, 245.
9. *Annales Bertiniani*: 30–33, s.a. 839. English translation by the author.
10. Duczko 2004: 54–56.
11. Monticolo 1890: 113–114. English translation by the author.
12. Pastorello 1938: 150. English translation by the author.
13. Monticolo 1890: 113–114; Vasiliev 1935: 182, n. 4.
14. For the function of the imperial *bestiarion*: Haldon 2000: 291.
15. Monticolo 1890: 115; see Trakadas, this volume, p. 82–85.
16. Thurn 1973: 79; Lesmüller-Werner & Thurn 1978: 50; Bekker 1838: 135; Shepard 1995: 46, n. 16.
17. Dölger 1956: 206–212 (text and likely chronology); Shepard 1995: 45–46. Description of the papyrus in Dölger 2009: 216, no. 413.
18. An alternative occasion for the despatch of the letter would be the delivery by a Byzantine embassy of a work of Pseudo-Dionysius the Areopagite to Louis the Pious in 827. The book survives (Cod. Par. gr. 437). M. McCormick made a case for this, pointing to the expedition mounted some months later by Count Boniface II of Tuscany, in quest of Muslim

pirates off Corsica and Sardinia; failing to find any, Boniface put in to Sardinia and picked up pilots to guide him to Africa, where he harried the coastline of the Gulf of Tunis: McCormick 2001: 264–265; 913, no. 404; McCormick 2005: 139, 146–149; Dölger 2009: 216, no. 413.
19. Nerlich 1999: 272; Dölger 2009: 228, no. 443. See also Schreiner 2011: 769, no. 47.
20. Bekker 1838: 135. English translation by the author.
21. Thurn 1973: 79. These events are also recorded by Joseph Genesios, see Lesmüller-Werner & Thurn 1978: 50–51.
22. *Annales Bertiniani*: 42, s.a. 842. English translation by the author.
23. Pastorello 1938: 151. English translation by the author.
24. See Shepard & Cheynet, this volume, pp. 88-89.
25. Reiske 1829: 674; Moffatt & Tall 2012: 673–674.
26. Reiske 1829: 660; Moffatt & Tall 2012: 660; Prigent 2010: 79–83.
27. The case for viewing Tissø as an occasional residence of the king was made by Jørgensen 2008: 77–82. See also Duczko 2004: 39–40, 56–58.
28. Bulgakova 2004: 53–55.
29. Shepard 1995: 44.

PP. 74–77
The sea of Venice: new cities and the Adriatic Mediterranean economy
SAURO GELICHI

1. Giovanni Diacono, *Istoria Veneticorum*, II, 50 (Berto 1999); see Shepard, this volume, pp. 68–73.
2. Hodges & Whitehouse 1983.
3. Hodges 1982: 24.
4. Gelichi & Hodges 2012.
5. Giovanni Diacono, *Istoria Veneticorum*, II, 29 (Berto 1999).
6. As mentioned in the earlier years by Cassiodorus, *Variæ*, 24.
7. McCormick 2007.
8. Theuws 2012: color plate 6.
9. Wickham 2005; Gelichi 2008.
10. Hodges 2012b: 232.
11. N. Cutajar, pers. comm.
12. Nef & Prigent 2010.
13. McCormick 2001: 832–833, A37–40.

PP. 78–81
Constantinople's Byzantine harbour: the Yenikapı excavations
UFUK KOCABAŞ

1. This Project is supported by Istanbul University's Scientific Research Projects Unit. Project numbers: 2294, 3907, 7381, 12765.
2. Gyllius 1997; Asal 2007; Gökçay 2007.
3. Kızıltan 2013; Kızıltan 2010.
4. Müller-Wiener 1998: 8-9.
5. Müller-Wiener 1998: 18.
6. Upon invitation by the Directorate of Istanbul Archaeology Museums, Dr. Ufuk Kocabaş has supervised the scientific research of 28 of the 37 shipwrecks; eight shipwrecks were turned over to Institute of Nautical Archaeology (INA) for study. See Kocabaş 2008; Kızıltan 2013.
7. Akkemik 2008: 201–212.
8. See Özsait-Kocabaş, this volume, pp. 86–87.
9. Özsait-Kocabaş 2011a: 137–148; Kocabaş 2012: 1-5.
10. Özsait-Kocabaş & Kocabaş 2008: 97–186.
11. Sakelliades 1997: 47–54; Pryor & Jeffreys 2006; Pulak 2007: 128–141; see Trakadas, this volume, pp. 82–85.
12. Kocabaş 2010: 23–33; Kocabaş et al. 2012.

PP. 82–85
A sea in transition: ships of the Mediterranean
ATHENA TRAKADAS

1. Agius 2008: 265-275; http://cudl.lib.cam.ac.uk/collections/genizah (accessed 1/2014); Pulak et al. 2013: 25-26.
2. Pomey et al. 2012.
3. Of the 37 wrecks from Yenikapı, 26 have presently been studied in more detail; of these, 10 have been preliminarily dated to fall within the 9th century. Kızıltan 2013; see Kocabaş, this volume, pp. 78–81.
4. Agius 2008: 355–357; Fahmy 1966: 27–42; Bell 1906.
5. Pulak et al. 2013: 29–30; Pomey et al. 2012.
6. Whitewright 2009.
7. For example, the Yenikapı 12 wreck is just under 10 m long (see Özsait-Kocabaş, this volume, pp. 86–87). There are exceptions and a few ships appear to be longer than 15 m (see Kocabaş, this volume, pp. 78–81); Harpster 2009; Pomey et al. 2012: 271–273.
8. Ahrweiler 1966: 409–410.
9. Theophanes, *Chronographia* 397; Ahrweiler 1966: 409.
10. Agius 2008: 27–272.
11. Cassiodorus, *Varia* 5.16; see also Kocabaş, this volume, pp. 78–81.
12. Fahmy 1966: 126–127; Agius 2008: 273–275, 334–338, 348–351.
13. Hocker 1995: 94–95.
14. Constatnine Porphyrogenitus, *De Caeremoniis* II, 45.
15. See Shepard, this volume, pp. 68–73.
16. Pryor 1988: 59–60.
17. Pulak et al. 2013: 26; see Kocabaş, this volume, pp.78–81.

PP. 86–87
The Yenikapı 12 wreck: connecting Constantinople
IŞIL ÖZAİT-KOCABAŞ

1. Kocabaş 2008. This project is supported by Istanbul University's Scientific Research Projects Unit. Project numbers: 1845.
2. Kocabaş 2012: 10.
3. Özsait-Kocabaş 2011b.
4. Özsait-Kocabaş 2012.
5. Asal 2007: 184.

PP. 88–89
The seals of Theodosios
JONATHAN SHEPARD & J.-C. CHEYNET

1. See Shepard, this volume, pp. 68–73.
2. For the characteristics of the seals of Byzantine officials, the imagery favoured, and the other types of persons who issued seals, see Cheynet 2008: 16–21, 36–41, 52-55, 72–74.
3. Laurent 1978: 36–40; Feveile & Jensen 2000: 14, fig. 7c; Feveile 2006, vol. 1.2: 144, pl. 53; Jørgensen 2002: 241, figs 10, 14, 15; Jørgensen 2008: 77–82; Duczko 2004: 39-40, 52–57.
4. Oikonomides 1986: no. 46.
5. Illustration in Cheynet 2008: 10, fig. 5.
6. See Whittow 1996: 1; Cheynet 2008: 8–12.
7. But this was obviously not the case with the Istanbul seal. As for the Danish and German seals, Theodosios could scarcely have counted on sealed bags and emissaries' promises alone to win over Horic and other Viking lords; see Cheynet 2008: 42.
8. Duczko 2004: 55, 170–171.

PP. 90–91
Theophilos' coin: treasure and image
HELLE HORSNÆS

1. Grierson 1982.
2. Wołoszyn 2009.
3. Fuglesang & Wilson 2006.
4. Georganteli & Cook 2006; see Shepard, this volume, pp. 68–73.

PP. 96–97
Kaupang: Viking-Age expansion to the North
UNN PEDERSEN

1. Bately & Englert 2007; see also Bately, this volume, pp. 14–20.
2. Skre 2007c.
3. Pedersen 2010.
4. Stylegar 2007.

PP. 98–99
Truso, silver and trade
MATEUSZ BOGUCKI

1. Hundreds of thousands of coins have been found, suggesting that millions were imported and either lost or melted down to form other objects. See Horsnæs, this volume, p. 65.
2. See Bately, this volume, pp. 14–20.
3. Jagodziński 2010.
4. Lewicki 1949: 352–353; Montgomery 2008.
5. Montgomery 2008.
6. Graham-Campbell et al. 2011; Bogucki & Rębkowski 2013.
7. Mongomery 2008.

PP. 100–101
The Inchmarnock 'Hostage Stone'
CHRIS LOWE

1. Bately & Englert 2007; see also Bately, this volume, pp. 14–20.
2. Holm 1986; Wyatt 2009.
3. Smyth 1977: 154–168.
4. Lowe 2008.
5. Whitelock 1996
6. *Annals of Ulster* s.a 870.
7. *Annals of Ulster* s.a 951.

PP. 102–103
Hedeby from the sea-side
SVEN KALMRING

1. Kalmring 2010; Crumlin-Pedersen 1997.
2. Kalmring 2010: n. 153, 102–103.
3. Kalmring 2010: 390–442, 443–450 and references therein.
4. See Sindbæk, this volume, pp. 21–25.
5. Willroth 1992: 444–458; Müller-Wille 2007.
6. Kalmring 2013.
7. Clarke & Ambrosiani 1993: 138.
8. See Bately, this volume, pp. 14–20.
9. Wulfstan: Paulus Orosius, *Historiarum adversum Paganos Libri Septem*; cf. Hilberg 2009; Gunnarr Hamundarson: *Njál's Saga*, Ch. 31; Cf. Hilberg & Kalmring in press; Ibrāhīm ibn Ya'qūb: Charvát 2000: 150; Theodosios: see Shepard & Cheynet, this volume, pp. 88–89.
10. Crumlin-Pedersen 1997: 141–143.

PP. 104–105
Making new money: the Hedeby coin
J.C. MOESGAARD & OLE KASTHOLM

1. Garipzanov 2008; Moesgaard 2008; Moesgaard & Uldum 2010.
2. Ploug 2012.
3. See Tys, this volume, pp. 34–35.
4. Malmer 1966.
5. Garipzanov 2008; Moesgaard 2008; Moesgaard & Uldum 2010.
6. See, i.e., Crumlin-Pedersen & Thye 1995.
7. Williams 2010.
8. Christensen 1964; Crumlin-Pedersen 1997: 174.
9. Andersen & Andersen 1989; Kastholm 2009; Kastholm 2011.
10. Cf. Varenius 1994.

PP. 106–107
Aylah, "Palestine's harbour on the China Sea"
KRISTOFFER DAMGAARD

1. Collins 2001: 149.
2. Whitcomb 1998; Whitcomb 2009; Damgaard 2009; Damgaard 2013.
3. Damgaard 2011.
4. Raith *et al.* 2013.
5. Aylah Archaeological Project, see Damgaard 2011; Damgaard 2012.

PP. 108–110
The world in a grain of sand: Siraf
SORNA KHAKZAD & ATHENA TRAKADAS

1. Le Strange 1966: 257–260, 295–298.
2. See Power, this volume, pp. 46–49.
3. De Goeje 1967: Vol. 4, 4.
4. It is not clear what is meant by 'China vessels' – if these are ships from China, or ships that sailed from the Indian Ocean to China (the latter recounted in Abhara's story), or both. Ferrand 1922: 18–19, 39; see Power, this volume, pp. 46–49.
5. Whitehouse 2001; Whitehouse 2009. See in this volume, Wynne-Jones, pp. 50–53; Sindbæk, pp. 121–123; Power, pp. 46–49.
6. De Goeje 1906; De Goeje 1927; Le Strange & Nicholson 1962: 158; Whitehouse 2009: 9–14.
7. Whitehouse & Williamson 1973; Whitehouse 2009: 8–12; Whitehouse 1980.
8. Kramers & Weit 1964: Vol. 2, 284–288.
9. De Goeje 1906: 96.
10. Whitehouse 2009.
11. Agius 2008: 79; Whitehouse 1983; Aubin 1959.

PP. 111–114
Zanzibar: a network society
STEPHANIE WYNNE-JONES, ALISON CROWTHER & MARK HORTON

1. Kramers & Wiet 1964.
2. Shepherd 1982.
3. Edson & Savage-Smith 2004.
4. See Agius, this volume, pp. 40–45.
5. Horton *forthcoming*; Juma 2004.
6. The lay-out of the site was recently investigated in a magnetometer survey undertaken in 2013 as part of the research project "ENTREPOT: Maritime Network Urbanism in Global Medieval Archaeology", organised in collaboration between Aarhus University, Denmark, and University of York, UK, funded 2012–2014 by a Sapere Aude grant from the Danish Council for Independent Research. See: http://projekter.au.dk/en/entrepot/.
7. See Wynne-Jones, this volume, pp. 50–53.
8. New evidence on the connections of Unguja Ukuu have emerged from excavations undertaken in 2012 within the research project "Sealinks – Bridging continents across the sea: Multidisciplinary perspectives on the prehistoric emergence of long-distance maritime contacts in the Indian Ocean", funded by a grant from the European Research Council (Agreement No. 206148). See Crowther *et al.* forthcoming.
9. See Wynne-Jones, this volume, pp. 50–53.

PP. 115–117
The Srivijaya Empire and its maritime aspects
JOHN MIKSIC

1. Takakusu 1896.
2. Wolters 1967.
3. Miksic 2013.
4. Geographers of the 9th and 10th centuries state that a journey from the Persian Gulf to China could take 120 days; then they would have to trade and wait for optimal weather to return to the Gulf – possibly taking, in the best conditions, at least 18 months. See Hourani 1995: 69–74; Whitewright, this volume, pp. 62–63.
5. See this volume, Vosmer, pp. 58–61; Khakzad & Trakadas, pp. 108–110.
6. Wheatley 1961; see also Agius, this volume, pp. 40–45.
7. Guillot 1998; Guillot *et al.* 2003; Manguin 1993b.
8. Wheatley 1961.
9. Wang 1958: 80; for information on early Arabo-Persian contacts with China, see Ma Wenkuan 2006; Rong 2011; Sen 1996.
10. 'Akhbār al-Ṣīn wa 'l-hind, 916 CE, in Renaudot 1733.
11. Bronson 1996.
12. Wheatley 1961: 59–60.
13. Wolters 1958: 101.
14. Wong 2010: 11 (Ch. 6); An 1984.

PP. 118–120
Seafaring in the Far East
JUN KIMURA

1. Hall 1985; see Miksic, this volume, pp. 115–117.
2. Miksic & Goh 2013.
3. Clarke *et al.* 1993.
4. Manguin 1993a.
5. McGrail 2001: 289–310. For other sewn boat traditions, see also Green & Trakadas, this volume, pp.54–57.
6. Yahya 2005.
7. Priyanto 2010.
8. Flecker 2012; Lacsina 2012.
9. Hourani 1995.
10. *Jewel of Muscat*, based on the Belitung shipwreck, found in Indonesian waters, recreated a portion of this historical trading sea route in 2010. In this volume, see Vosmer, pp.58–61; Power, pp. 46–49.

PP. 121–123
Suzhou, China, and the Maritime Silk Road
SØREN M. SINDBÆK

1. Wang 2003.
2. Krahl 2010: 49.
3. See Power, this volume, pp. 46–49.
4. Krahl 2010.
5. Lu 1974.
6. Ho 1994.
7. Manguin 1993b: 34; Li 2006.
8. See Vosmer, this volume, pp. 58–61.
9. Bynner & Chiang 1960.

PP. 124–125
The journey of ideas
SØREN M. SINDBÆK & ATHENA TRAKADAS

1. Wink 2002: 78–86; see Wynne-Jones, this volume, pp. 50–53.
2. Déroche 1992: 1–25.
3. See Miksic, this volume, pp. 115–117.
4. Alpers 2014: 34–36.
5. Hall 2011: 65.
6. Gräslund 2001: 129; Feveile 2011; Zachrisson 2012; Ambrosiani 2013: 240.
7. Shetelig 1950; Sindbæk 2014.

References

A

Adams, R.M. 1965: *The Land behind Baghdad: A History of Settlement on the Diyala Plains.* Chicago.

Adams, R.M. 1981: *Heartland of Cities: Surveys of Ancient Settlement and Land Use on the Central Floodplain of the Euphrates.* Chicago.

Agius, D. 2008: *Classic ships of Islam: From Mesopotamia to the Indian Ocean.* Leiden.

Ahrweiler, H. 1966: *Byzance et la mer. La marine de guerre la politique et la institutions maritimes de Byzance aux VIIe–XVe siècles.* Paris.

Akkemik, Ü. 2008: VII. Identification of timbers from Yenikapı 12 shipwreck / VII. Yenikapı 12 batığı ahşaplarının cins/tür teşhisleri, in U. Kocabaş 2008: 201–211.

Alpers, E.A. 2014: *The Indian Ocean in World History.* Oxford.

Ambrosiani, B. 2013: *Excavations in the Black Earth 1990–1995. Stratigraphy Vol. 1. Part One: The Site and the Shore. Part Two: The Bronze Caster's Workshop.* Stockholm.

Ambrosiani, B. & Clarke, H. 1995: *Towns in the Viking Age.* London.

Andersen, B. & Andersen, E. 1989: *Råsejlet – Dragens Vinge.* Roskilde.

Andersen, E. 1995: Woollen material for sails, in O. Olsen, J. Skamby Madsen & F. Rieck (eds), *Shipshape. Essays for Ole Crumlin-Pedersen on the occasion of his 60th anniversary February 24th 1995*, 249–270. Roskilde.

Andersen, E. & Nørgård, A. 2009: *Et uldsejl til Oselven. Arbejdsrapport om fremstillingen af et uldsejl til en traditionel vestnorsk båd.* Roskilde.

Andersen, M. 1895: *Vikingefærden. En illustreret Beskrivelse af "Vikings" Reise i 1893.* Kristiania.

Andersson, E. 2003: *Tools for textile production from Birka to Hedeby: excavations in the Black Earth 1990–1995.* Stockholm.

An Jiayao 1984: Zhongguo de zaoqi bolli qimin [The early glass vessels of China]. *Acta Archaeologica Sinica* 4: 413–447.

Annales Bertiniani: Grat, F., Vielliard, J. & Clémencet, S. (eds) 1964: *Annales de Saint-Bertin.* Paris.

Asal, R. 2007: İstanbul'un ticareti ve Theodosius Limanı, in Karamani Pekin & Kangal 2007: 180–189.

Ashby, S.P. 2009: Combs, contact, and chronology: reconsidering hair combs in Early-historic and Viking-Age Atlantic Scotland. *Medieval Archaeology* 53: 1–33.

Ashby, S.P. 2011: An atlas of medieval combs from northern Europe. *Internet Archaeology* 30. http://intarch.ac.uk/journal/issue30/ashby_index.html (accessed November, 2013).

Ashby, S.P., Coutu, A. & Sindbæk, S.M. in prepration: Arctic outlands, urban markets and long-distance journeys: Tracking Viking-age maritime expansion through the presence of reindeer antler in southern Scandinavia.

Aubin, J. 1959: La Ruine de Siraf et les Routes du Golfe Persique aux XIe et XIIe siècles. *Cahiers de Civilisation Médiévale* 2: 295–301.

Auzépy, M.-F. 2008: State of emergency (700–850), in J. Shepard (ed.), *The Cambridge History of the Byzantine Empire, c. 500–1492*, 251–291. Cambridge.

B

Barbier de Meynard, C. & de Courteille, A. (trans.) 1861, 1864: Ali 'ibn al-Husain al-Ma'sudi, *Les Prairies d'Or*, Vols. II, III. Paris.

Barrett, J.H. 2008: What caused the Viking Age? *Antiquity* 82: 671–685.

Barrett, J.H., Orton, D., Johnstone, C., Harland, J., Van Neer, W., Ervynck, A., Roberts, C., Locker, A., Amundsen, C., Bødker Enghoff, I., Hamilton-Dyer, S., Heinrich, D., Hufthammer, A.K., Jones, A.K.G., Jonsson, L., Makowiecki, D., Pope, P., O'Connell, T.C., de Roo, T. & Richards, M. 2011: Interpreting the expansion of sea fishing in medieval Europe using stable isotope analysis of archaeological cod bones. *Journal of Archaeological Science* 38: 1516–1524.

Bately, J. (ed.) 1980: *The Old English Orosius.* Oxford.

Bately, J. (ed.) 1986: MS A. The Anglo-Saxon Chronicle, a Collaborative Edition 3. Cambridge.

Bately, J. 2007: The Source, in Bately & Englert (eds) 2007: 18–58.

Bately, J. 2009: Wulfstan's voyage and his description of Estland: the text and the language of the text, in Englert & Trakadas 2009: 14–28.

Bately, J. & Englert, A. (eds) 2007: *Ohthere's Voyages. A late 9th-century account of voyages along the coasts of Norway and Denmark and its cultural context.* Roskilde.

Becker, C. & Grupe, G. 2012: Archaeometry meets archaeozoology: Viking Haithabu and medieval Schleswig reconsidered. *Journal of Archaeological Science* 39: 241–262.

Bekker, I. (ed.) 1838: Theophanes Continuatus, *Chronographia.* Bonn.

Bell, H.I. 1906: The Aphrodito Papyri. *The Journal of Hellenic Studies* 28: 97–120.

Berto, L.A. (trans.) 1999: Giovanni Diacono, *Istoria Veneticorum.* Bologna.

Binns, A.L. 1961: Ohtheriana VI: Ohthere's Northern Voyage. *English and Germanic Studies* 7: 43–52.

Bogucki, M. & Rębkowski, M. (eds) 2013: *Economies, Monetisation and Society in West Slavic Lands 800–1200 AD.* Wolin, Szczecin.

Bonde, N. 1994: De norske vikingeskibsgraves alder. Et vellykket norsk-dansk forskningsprojekt. *Nationalmuseets Arbejdsmark* 1994: 128–148.

Bonde, N. & Stylegar, F-A. 2009: Fra Avaldsnes til Oseberg. Dendrokronologiske undersøkelser av skipsgravene fra Storhaug og Grønhaug på Karmøy. *Viking.Norsk arkeologisk årbok* 72: 149–168.

Boussac, M.-F. & Salles, J.-F. (eds) 1995: *Athens, Aden, Arikamed: Essays on the interrelations between India, Arabia and the Eastern Mediterranean.* New Delhi.

Bracker, J., Henn, V. & Postel, R. 1999: *Die Hanse – Lebenswirklichkeit und Mythos.* Lübeck.

Brink, S. 2007: Geography, Toponymy and Political Organisation in Early Scandinavia, in Bately & Englert 2007: 66–73.

Broadhurst, R.J.C. (trans.) 1952: *Rihla. The Travels of Ibn Jubayr.* London.

Bronson, B. 1996: Chinese and Middle Eastern trade in Southern Thailand during the 9th century A.D. *Ancient Trades and Cultural Contacts in Southeast Asia*, 181–200. Bangkok.

Bulgakova, V. 2004: *Byzantinische Bleisiegel in Osteuropa. Die Funde auf dem Territorium Altrusslands.* Wiesbaden.

Bynner, W. & Chiang, K. (trans.) 1960: *The jade mountain.* New York.

C

Callmer, J. 1995: The influx of oriental beads into Europe during the 8th century, in M. Rasmussen, U. Lund Hansen & U. Näsman (eds), *Glass beads – Cultural History, Technology, Experiment and Analogy. Proceedings of the Nordic Glass Bead Seminar 16th–18th October 1992*, 49–54. Lejre.

Callmer, J. 2002: North-European trading centres and the early medieval craftsman. Craftsmen at Åhus, north-eastern Scania, Sweden ca. AD 750–850+, in B. Hårdh & L. Larsson (eds), *Central Places in the Migration and Merovingian Periods. Papers from the 52nd Sachsensymposium*, 133–158. Lund.

Callmer, J. 2007: Urbanisation in Northern and Eastern Europe ca. AD 700–1100, in J. Henning (ed.), *Post-Roman Towns, Trade and Settlement in Europe and Byzantium. Vol. 1 The Heirs of the Roman West*, 233–270. Berlin, New York.

Casson, L. 1989: *The Periplus Maris Erythraei: Text With Introduction, Translation, and Commentary.* Princeton, NJ.

Charvát, P. 2000: Gesandtschaften, Pilgerfahrten und Reiseberichte, in A. Wieczorek & H.-M. Hinz (eds), Europas Mitte um 1000. Handbuch zur Ausstellung 1, 148–151. Stuttgart.

Chaudhuri, K.N. 1985: Trade and Civilization in the Indian Ocean. An Economic History from the Rise of Islam to 1750. Cambridge.

Cheynet, J.-C. 2008: Introduction à la sigillographie byzantine, in J.-C. Cheynet, La société byzantine. L'apport des sceaux, I, 1–82. Paris.

Chittick, H.N. 1984: Manda: Excavations at an Island Port on the Kenya Coast. Nairobi, London.

Christensen, A.E. 1964: Birka-Hedeby myntene som kilde til skipets historie på 800-tallet. Norsk Sjøfartsmuseum 1914–1964. Museets historie, skipsstudier; årsberetning for 1963, 81–86. Oslo.

Christensen, A.E. 1998: Skipsrestene fra Storhaug og Grønhaug, in A. Opedal (ed.), De glemte skipsgravene. Makt og myter på Avaldsnes, 206–220. Stavanger.

Christensen, A.E. 2007: Ohthere's Vessel, in Bately & Englert 2007: 112–116.

Clark, P., Green, J., Vosmer, T. & Santiago, R. 1993: The Butuan two boat known as a balangay in the National Museum, Manila, Philippines. The International Journal of Nautical Archaeology 22.2: 143–159.

Clarke, H. & Ambrosiani, B. 1993: Vikingastäder. Höganäs.

Collins, B. (trans.) 2001. The Best Divisions for Knowledge of the Regions. Ahsan al-Taqāsîm fi Ma'rifat al-Aqālim by Al-Muqaddasî. Reading.

Crowther, A., Horton, M. & Boivin, N. forthcoming: Zanzibar's Ancient Indian Ocean Trade and Contacts: Studies at Unguja Ukuu and Fukuchani. Oxford.

Crumlin-Pedersen, O. 1997: Viking-Age Ships and Shipbuilding in Hedeby/Haithabu and Schleswig. Schleswig, Roskilde.

Crumlin-Pedersen, O. 1999: Ships as indicators of trade in Northern Europe 600–1200, in J. Bill & B.L. Clausen (eds), Maritime Topography and the Medieval Town, 11–20. Copenhagen.

Crumlin-Pedersen, O. 2010: Archaeology and the Sea in Scandinavia and Britain. A personal account. Roskilde.

Crumlin-Pedersen, O. & B.M. Thye (eds) 1995: The Ship as Symbol. Copenhagen.

D

Dāghir, Y.A. (ed.) 1983: Abū l-Ḥasan ʿAlī b. Al-Ḥusayn Al-Masʿūdī, Murūj al-dhahab wa-maʿādin al-jawhar (The Golden Meadows and Mines of Precious Stones), Vols. I–IV. Beirut.

Damgaard, K. 2009. A Palestinian Red Sea Port on the Egyptian Road to Arabia: Early Islamic Aqaba and its many hinterlands, in L. Blue, J. Cooper, R. Thomas & J. Whitewright (eds), Connected Hinterlands: Proceedings of the Red Sea Project IV held at the University of Southampton, September 2008, 85–97. Oxford.

Damgaard, K. 2011. MARE OECONOMICUS. Ny dansk forskning i rødehavsregionen. Tværkultur 2: 99–108.

Damgaard, K. 2012. Aqaba – Jordans Historiske Havneby. SFINX 35.2: 72–77.

Damgaard, K. 2013. Between Castrum and Medina: A preliminary note on spatial organisation and urban development in Medieval Aqaba, in U. Vermeulen, J. V. Steenbergen & K. D'hulster (eds), Egypt and Syria in the Fatimid, Ayyubid and Mamluk Eras VII, 39–65. Leuven.

Dammann, W. 1996 (2nd edn): Das Gokstadschiff und seine Boote. Brilon-Gudenhagen.

De Goeje, M.J. (ed.) 1892: al-Ya'qubi, Kitāb al-buldān. Leiden.

De Goeje, M.J. (ed.) 1906 (2nd edn): Muḥammad b. Aḥmad Al-Muqaddasī, Aḥsan al-taqāsīm fī maʿrifat al-aqālim (The Best Divisions for Knowledge of the Regions). Leiden.

De Goeje, M.J. (ed.) 1927 (2nd edn): Abū Isḥāq Ibrāhīm b. Muḥammad Al-Iṣṭakhrī, Kitāb masālik al-mamālik (The Book of Routes and Provinces). Leiden.

De Goeje, M.J. (ed.) 1967 (3rd edn): ʿUbayd Allāh Ibn Khurradādhbih, Kitāb al-masālik wa l-mamālik (The Book of Roads and Kingdoms). Leiden.

Deloche, J. 1980: Transport and Communications in India prior to steam locomotion. Volume 2: Water transport. Oxford.

Déroche, F. 1992: The Abbasid Tradition: Qur'ans of the 8th to the 10th Centuries A.D., The Nasser D. Khalili Collection of Islamic Art, Vol. 1. Oxford.

Dölger, F. 1956: Der Pariser Papyrus von St. Denis als ältestes Kreuzzugsdokument. Reprinted in F. Dölger, Byzantinische Diplomatik, 204–214. Ettal.

Dölger, F. 2009: Regesten der Kaiserurkunden des oströmischen Reiches, I.1. Munich.

Duczko, W. 2004: Viking Rus. Studies on the Presence of Scandinavians in Eastern Europe. Leiden.

E

Edson, E. & Savage-Smith, E. 2004: Medieval Views of the Cosmos. Oxford.

Elders, J. 2001: The lost churches of the Arabian Gulf: recent discoveries on the islands of Sir Bani Yas and Marawah, Abu Dhabi Emirate, United Arab Emirates. Proceedings of the Seminar for Arabian Studies 31: 47–57.

Ellmers, D. 1999: Welche Schiffstypen stellen die Haithabu-Münzen des frühen 9. Jahrdunderts dar? Offa 56: 367–373.

Englert, A. 2007: Ohthere's Voyages seen from a nautical angle, in Bately & Englert 2007: 117–129.

Englert, A. & Trakadas, A. (eds) 2009: Wulfstan's Voyage. The Baltic Sea region in the early Viking Age as seen from shipboard. Roskilde.

Eshragh, S. 2010: Silver coinage of the Caliphs. London.

F

Fahmy, A.M. 1966: Muslim naval organization in the eastern Mediterranean: from the seventh to tenth centuries AD. Cairo.

Ferrand, G. (trans.) 1922: Voyage du marchand arabe Sulaymān en Inde et en Chine, Rédigé en 851, Suivi de Remarques par Abū Zayd Ḥasan (c. 916). Paris.

Feveile, C. (ed.) 2006: Det ældste Ribe. Udgravninger på nordsiden af Ribe Å 1984–2000. Aarhus.

Feveile, C. 2011: Korsfibler af Råhedetypen. En upåagtet fibeltype fra ældre vikingetid, Kuml – Årbog for Jysk Arkæologisk Selskab 2011: 143–160.

Feveile, C. & Jensen, S. 2000: Ribe in the 8th and 9th century. A contribution to the archaeological chronology of North Western Europe, in S. Stummann Hansen & K. Randsborg (eds), Vikings in the West, 9–24. Copenhagen.

Flecker, M. 2012: The Jade dragon wreck: Sabah, East Malaysia. The Mariner's Mirror 98.1: 9–29.

Fleisher, J. & LaViolette, A. 2013: The Early Swahili Trade Village of Tumbe, Pemba Island, Tanzania, AD 600–950. Antiquity: 1151–1168.

Fleisher, J. & Wynne-Jones, S. 2011: Ceramics and the Early Swahili. African Archaeological Review 28.4: 245–278.

Foulke, W.D. (trans.) & Peters, E. (ed.) 2003: History of the Langobards. Philadelphia.

Francis, P. 2002: Asia's Maritime Bead Trade, 300 B.C. to the Present. Honolulu.

Franklin, S. & Shepard, J. 1996: The Emergence of Rus, 700–1200. London.

Freeman-Grenville, G.S.P. (trans. & ed.) 1981: Buzurg Ibn Shahriyār al-Ramhormuzi, The Book of the Wonders of India: Mainland, Sea and Islands. London, the Hague.

Fuglesang, S.H. & Wilson, D. (eds) 2006: The Hoen hoard: a Viking gold treasure of the ninth century. Oslo.

G

Galland, A. (trans.) 1704–1717: Les Mille et une nuits, Vols. 1–12. Paris.

Garipzanov, I. 2008: Carolingian Coins in Early Viking Age Scandinavia (c.754–c.900): Chronological Distribution and Regional Patterns. Nordisk Numismatisk Årsskrift 2003–2005: 65–92.

Garlake, P.S. & Garlake, M. 1964: Early ship engravings of the East African coast. Tanganyika Notes and Records 63: 197–206.

Gelichi, S. 2008: The eels of Venice. The long eighth century of the emporia of northern region along the Adriatic coast, in S. Gasparri (ed.), 774. Ipotesi su una transizione, Poggibonsi 2006, 81–117. Turnhout.

Gelichi, S. & Hodges, R. (eds) 2012: From one sea to another. Trading places in the European and Mediterranean Early Middle Ages. Proceedings of the International Conference, Comacchio 27th–29th March 2009. Turnhout.

Gelling, M. & Cole, A. 2000: *The Landscape of Place-Names*. Stamford.

Georganteli, E. & Cook, B. 2006: *Encounters. Travel and Money in the Byzantine World*. London.

Gerhardt, M.L. 1963: *The Art of Story-Telling; A Literary Study of the Thousand and One Nights*. Leiden.

Gernet, J. 1982: *A History of Chinese Civilisation*. Cambridge.

Ghosh, A. 1990: *An Encyclopaedia of Indian Archaeology*, Vols. 1–2. Leiden.

Gökçay, M. 2007: Yenikapı kazılarında ortaya çıkarılan mimari buluntular, in Karamani Pekin & Kangal 2007: 167–179.

Goodacre, S., Helgason, A., Nicholson, J., Southam, L., Ferguson, L., Hickey, E., Vega, E., Stefánsson, K., Ward, R. & Sykes, B. 2005: Genetic evidence for a family-based Scandinavian settlement of Shetland and Orkney during the Viking periods. *Heredity* 95: 129–135.

Graham-Campbell, J., Sindbæk, S.M. & Williams, G. (eds) 2011: *Silver Economies, Monetisation and Society in Scandinavia, AD 800–1100*. Aarhus.

Gräslund, A.-S. 2001: *Ideologi och Mentalitet – om religionsskiftet i Skandinavien från en arkeologisk horisont*. Uppsala.

Grierson, P. 1982: *Byzantine Coins*. London.

Guillot, C. (ed.) 1998: *Histoire de Barus: Le Site de Lobu Tua. I. Études et Documents*. Paris.

Guillot, C., Dupoizat, M.-F., Perret, D., Sunaryo, U. & Surachman, H. (eds) 2003: *Histoire de Barus Sumatra. Le Site de Lobu Tua. II. Étude archéologique et Documents*. Paris.

Guy, J. 2001–2002: Early Asian ceramic trade and the Belitung ('Tang') cargo. *Transactions of the Oriental Ceramics Society* 66: 13–27.

Gyllius, P. 1997: *İstanbul'un Tarihi Eserleri*. Istanbul.

H

Haldon, J.F. 2000: Theory and practice in tenth-century military administration. *Travaux et Mémoires* 13: 201–352.

Hall, E. 2008: *The Return of Ulysses: A Cultural History of Homer's Odyssey*. London.

Hall, K.R. 1985: *Maritime trade and state development in early Southeast Asia*. Honolulu.

Hall, K.R. 2011: *A history of early Southeast Asia. Maritime trade and societal development, 100–1500*. Lanham, MD.

Harpster, M. 2009: Designing the 9th-century AD vessel from Bozburun, Turkey. *The International Journal of Nautical Archaeology* 38.2: 297–313.

Haywood, J. 1991: *Dark Age Naval Power. A re-assessment of Frankish and Anglo-Saxon seafaring activity*. London, New York.

Heikell, R. 1999: *Indian Ocean Cruising Guide*. St. Ives.

Hilberg, V. 2009: Hedeby in Wulfstan's days: a Danish emporium of the Viking Age between East and West, in Englert & Trakadas 2009: 79–113.

Hilberg, V. & Kalmring, S. in press: Viking Age Hedeby and Its Relations with Iceland and the North Atlantic. Communication, Long-distance Trade and Production, in D. Zori & J. Byock (eds), *Viking Age Archaeology in Iceland: The Mosfell Archaeological Project*. Turnhout.

Hirth, F. & Rockhill, W.W. (trans. & annotated) 1911: *Chau Ju-Kua, his work on the Chinese and Arab Trade in the 12th and 13th centuries, entitled 'Chu-fan-chi'*. St. Petersburg.

Hitti, P. 1970 (10th edn): *A History of the Arabs from the Earliest Times to the Present*. London, New York.

Ho, C. 1994: *New light on Chinese Yue and Longquan wares: archaeological ceramics found in eastern and southern Asia, A.D. 800–1400*. Hong Kong.

Hocker, F.M. 1995: Late Roman, Byzantine, and Islamic galleys and fleets, in R. Gardiner (ed.), *The age of the galley: Mediterranean oared vessels since pre-Classical times*, 86–100. Bath.

Hodges, R. 1982: *Dark Age Economics*. London.

Hodges R. 2012a: *Dark Age Economics Revisited: A New Audit*. London.

Hodges, R. 2012b: Adriatic Sea Trade in an European perspective, in S. Gelichi & R. Hodges (eds), *From one sea to another. Trading places in the European and Mediterranean Early Middle Ages. Proceedings of the International Conference, Comacchio 27th–29th March 2009*, 207–234. Turnhout.

Hodges, R. & Whitehouse, D. 1983: *Muhammad, Charlemagne and the Origins of Europe: Archaeology and the Pirenne Thesis*. London.

Holm, I., Innselset, S. & Øye, I. (eds) 2005: *'Utmark'. The Outfield as Industry and Ideology in the Iron Age and the Middle Ages*. Bergen.

Holm, P. 1986: The slave trade of Dublin, ninth to twelfth centuries. *Peritia* 5: 317–345.

von Holstein, I.C.C, Ashby, S.P., van Doorn, N.L., Sachs, S.M., Buckley, M., Meiri, M., Barnes, I., Brundle, A., & Collins, M.J. 2014: Searching for Scandinavians in pre-Viking Scotland: molecular fingerprinting of Early Medieval combs. *Journal of Archaeological Science* 41: 1–6.

Horden, P., & Purcell, N. 2000: *The corrupting sea: A study of Mediterranean history*. Oxford.

Horsnæs, H.W. & Ingvardson, G.T. forthcoming: A missing link – the Skovsholm Hoard and its contexts.

Horton, M. 1996: *Shanga: the archaeology of a Muslim trading community on the coast of East Africa*. London, Nairobi.

Horton, M.C. forthcoming: *Zanzibar and Pemba*. London.

Hourani, G.F. 1995 (2nd edn): *Arab seafaring in the Indian Ocean in ancient and early medieval times*. Princeton, NJ.

I

Imer, L.M. 2004: Gotlandske billedsten – dateringen af Lindqvists gruppe C og D. *Aarbøger for Nordisk Oldkyndighed og Historie* 2001: 47–111.

Insoll, T. 2003: *The Archaeology of Islam in Sub-Saharan Africa*. Cambridge.

Insoll, T. & Bahn, K. 2001: Carnelian Mines in Gujarat. *Antiquity* 75.289: 495–496.

Insoll, T., Polya, D., Bhan, K., Irving, D. & Jarvis, K. 2004: Towards an understanding of the carnelian bead trade from Western India to sub-Saharan Africa: The Application of UV-LA-ICP-MS to Carnelian from Gujarat, India, and West Africa. *Journal of Archaeological Science* 34.8: 1161–1173.

Irwin, R. 1994: *The Arabian Nights: A Companion*. London.

J

Jagodziński, M. 2010: *Truso. Between Weonodland and Witland*. Elbląg.

Jónsson, F. (trans. & ed.) 1926: *Kongespejlet. Konungs Skuggsjá i dansk oversættelse ved Finnur Jónsson*. Copenhagen.

Jørgensen, L. 2002: Kongsgård – kultsted – marked. Overvejelser omkring Tissøkompleksets struktur og function, in K. Jennbert, A. Andrén & C. Raudvere (eds), *Vägar till Midgård 2. Plats och praxis – Studier av nordisk förkristen ritual*, 215–247. Lund.

Jørgensen, L. 2008: Manor, cult and market at Lake Tissø, in S. Brink & N. Price (eds), *The Viking world*, 77–82. London.

Juma, A. 2004: *Unguja Ukuu on Zanzibar: An Archaeological Study of Ancient Urbanism*. Uppsala.

K

Kalmring, S. 2010: *Der Hafen von Haithabu*. Neumünster.

Kalmring, S. 2013: Vom Nordatlantik an die Schlei. Neu identifizierte Schiffsausrüstungsteile aus Haithabu und Schleswig. *Germania* 89: 305–328.

Karamani Pekin, A. & Kangal, S. (eds) 2007: *Gün Işığında: İstanbul'un 8000 Yılı. Marmaray, Metro ve Sultanahmet Kazıları*. Istanbul.

Kastholm, O.T. 2009: De gotlandske billedsten og rekonstruktionen af vikingeskibenes sejl. *Aarbøger for Nordisk Oldkyndighed og Historie* 2005: 99–159.

Kastholm, O.T. 2011: The rigging of the Viking Age warship. The Skuldelev find and the ship motifs, in L. Boye (ed.), *The Iron Age of Zealand. Status and Perspectives*, 175–183. Copenhagen.

Kennedy, H. (2nd edn) 2004: *The Prophet and the Age of the Caliphates: The Islamic Near East from the Sixth to the Eleventh Century*. Harlow.

Kershaw, J. 2013: *Viking Identities: Scandinavian jewellery in England*. Oxford.

Keynes, S. & Lapidge, M. 1983: *Alfred the Great: Asser's Life of King Alfred and other contemporary sources*. London.

Kızıltan, Z. 2010: Marmaray-Metro Projeleri Kapsamında Yapılan Yenikapı, Sirkeci ve Üsküdar Kazıları / Excavations at Yenikapı, Sirkeci and Üsküdar within Marmaray and Metro Projects, in Kocabaş 2010: 1–16.

Kızıltan, Z. (ed.) 2013: *Stories from the Hidden Harbour. Shipwrecks of Yenikapı.* Istanbul.

Kocabaş, U. (ed.) 2008: *Yenikapı Shipwrecks, Volume 1: Old Shipwrecks of New Gate 1 / Yenikapı Batıkları, Cilt 1: Yenikapı'nın Eski Gemileri 1.* Istanbul.

Kocabaş, U. (ed.) 2010: *İstanbul Arkeoloji Müzeleri Marmaray – Metro Kurtarma Kazıları Sempozyumu Bildiriler Kitabı, 5–6 Mayıs 2008 / Istanbul Archaeological Museums, Proceedings of the 1st Symposium on Marmaray-Metro Salvage Excavations 5th–6th May 2008.* Istanbul.

Kocabaş, U. 2012: The Latest Link in the Long Tradition of Maritime Archaeology in Turkey: The Yenikapı Shipwrecks. *European Journal of Archaeology* 15.1: 1–15.

Kocabaş, U., Özsait-Kocabaş, I. & Kılıç, N. 2012: The Yenikapı Shipwrecks: Dismantling Methods and First Step to Conservation, in K. Strætkvern & E. Williams (eds), *11th ICOM International Conference on Wet Organic Archaeological Materials (ICOM-WOAM)*, 303–312. Greenville, NC.

Kovalev, R. & Kaelin, A.C. 2007: Circulation of Arab Silver in Medieval Afro-Eurasia. *History Compass* 5.2: 560–580.

Krahl, R. 2010: Chinese Ceramics in the Late Tang Dynasty, in Krahl et al. 2010: 45–73.

Krahl, R., Guy, J., Wilson, J.K. & Raby, J. (eds) 2010: *Shipwrecked. Tang treasures and monsoon winds.* Singapore, Washington, D.C.

Kramers, J.H. & Weit, G. (trans.) 1964: Ibn Hawqal, *Configuration de la terre (Kitab surat al-ard).* Paris.

Kusimba, C.M. 1996: The Social Context of Iron Forging on the Kenya Coast, Africa. *Journal of the International African Institute* 66.3. 386–410.

Kusimba, C. 1999: *The Rise and Fall of Swahili States.* Walnut Creek, CA.

L

Lacsina, L.S.P. 2010: Traditional island Southeast Asian watercraft in Philippine archaeological sites, in M. Staniforth, J. Craig, S.C. Jago-on, B. Orillaneda & L. Lacsina (eds), *Proceedings on the Asia-Pacific Regional Conference on Underwater Cultural Heritage*, 787–798. Manila.

Latham, R. (trans.) 1958: *The travels of Marco Polo.* London.

Laurent, V. 1978: Ein byzantinische Bleisiegel aus Haithabu. *Berichte über die Ausgrabungen in Haithabu* 12, 36–40. Neumünster.

Laursen, R. 2013: Dirhemskat fra 800-tallet fundet på Bornholm. *Nordisk Numismatisk Unions Medlemsblad* 1: 16–19.

LaViolette, A. 2008: Swahili Cosmopolitanism in Africa and the Indian Ocean World, A.D. 600–1500. *Archaeologies: Journal of the World Archaeological Congress* 1: 24–49.

LaViolette, A. & Fleisher, J.B. 2009: The Urban History of a Rural Place: Swahili Archaeology on Pemba Island, Tanzania, 700–1500 AD. *International Journal of African Historical Studies* 42.3: 433–455.

Lesmüller-Werner, A. & Thurn, H. (eds) 1978: Joseph Genesios, *Regum Libri Quattuor.* Berlin, New York.

Le Strange, G. 1966: *The Lands of the Eastern Caliphate.* London.

Le Strange, G. & Nicholson, R.A. (eds) 1962: Ibn al-Balkhi, *The Fársnáma.* London.

Lewicki, T. 1949: Świat słowiański w oczach pisarzy arabskich. *Slavia Antiqua* 2: 321–388.

Li, Q. 2006: *Maritime silk road.* Beijing.

Lilie, R.-J., Ludwig, C., Pratsch T. & Rochow, I. 1998–2002: *Prosopographie der mittelbyzantinischen Zeit, Erste Abteilung (641–867)*, Vols. 1–5. Berlin, New York.

Lindqvist, S., Gustafson, G. & Nordin, F. 1941: *Gotlands Bildsteine.* Stockholm.

Losiński, W. 1988: Chronologia napływu monet arabskich na terytorium Europy. *Slavia Antiqua* 31: 93–181.

Loveluck, C. & Tys, D. 2006: Coastal societies, exchange and identity along the Channel and southern North Sea shores of Europe, AD 600–1000. *Journal of Maritime Archaeology* 1.2: 140–169.

Lowe, C.E. 2008: *Inchmarnock: an Early Historic Island Monastery and its archaeological landscape.* Edinburgh.

Lu, Y. 1974: *The classic of tea.* Boston.

Lunde, P. & Stone, C. (trans.) 2007: Al-Mas'udi, *From the Meadows of Gold.* London.

M

Makarov, N.A. 2007: The land of the Beormas, in Bately & Englert 2007: 140–149.

Malmer, B. 1966: *Nordiska mynt före 1000.* Lund, Bonn.

Manguin, P.-Y. 1993a: Trading ships of the South China Sea: shipbuilding techniques and their role in the history of the development of Asian trade networks. *The Journal of the Economic and Social History of the Orient* 36.3: 253–280.

Manguin, P.-Y. 1993b: Palembang and Sriwijaya: an early Malay Harbour-City rediscovered. *Journal of the Malaysian Branch of the Royal Asiatic Society* 66:1: 23–46.

Manzano Moreno, E. 1998: Byzantium and al-Andalus in the ninth century, in L. Brubaker (ed.), *Byzantium in the Ninth Century: Dead or Alive?*, 215–227. Aldershot.

Ma Wenkuan, A. 2006: *The Discovery of and Research on the Islamic Cultural Relics Found in China.* Beijing.

McCormick, M. 2001: *Origins of European Economy. Communications and Commerce AD 300–900.* Cambridge.

McCormick, M. 2005: La lettre diplomatique byzantine du premier millénaire vue de l'Occident et l'énigme du papyrus de Paris, in M. Balard, E. Malamut & J.-M. Spieser (eds), *Byzance et le monde extérieur*, 135–149. Paris.

McCormick, M. 2007: Where do trading towns come from? Early medieval Venice and the northern emporia, in J. Henning (ed.), *Post-Roman towns, trade and settlement in Europe and Byzantium. Vol. I. The heirs of the Roman West*, 41–68. Berlin.

McGrail, S. 2001: *Boats of the world: from the Stone Age to Medieval Times.* Oxford.

Miksic, J.N. 2013: *Singapore and the Silk Road of the Sea.* Singapore.

Miksic, J.N. & Goh, G.Y. (eds) 2013: *Ancient harbours in Southeast Asia: The archaeology of early harbours and evidence of inter-regional trade.* Bangkok.

Moesgaard, J.C. 2008: Udbredelsen af reguleret møntøkonomi i geografisk perspektiv ca. 600–ca. 1150. *Hikuin* 35: 133–150.

Moesgaard, J.C. & Uldum, O. 2010: Havsmarken, in M. Andersen & P.O. Nielsen (eds), *Danefæ, skatte fra den danske muld*, 165–169. Copenhagen.

Moffatt, A. & Tall, M. (trans.) 2012: *Constantine Porphyrogennetos, The Book of Ceremonies*, II. Canberra.

Montgomery, J.E. 2008: Arabic sources on the Vikings, in S. Brink & N. Price (eds), *Viking World*, 550–561. London, New York.

Monticolo, G. (ed.) 1890: John the Deacon, *Cronaca Veneziana*, in G. Monticolo (ed.), *Cronache Veneziane antichissime.* Rome.

Mott, L.V. 1997: *The development of the rudder, a technological tale.* College Station, TX.

Müller-Wiener, W. 1998: *Bizans'tan Osmanlı'ya İstanbul Limanı.* Istanbul.

Müller-Wille, M. 2007: Hedeby in Ohthere's Time, in Bately & Englert 2007: 157–165.

Müller-Wille, M. 2009: Summary, in Englert & Trakadas 2009: 356–363.

Munch, G.S., Johansen, O.S. & Roesdahl, E. (eds) 2003: *Borg in Lofoten. A chieftain's farm in North Norway.* Trondheim.

N

Nef, A. & V. Prigent (eds) 2010: *La Sicile de Byzance à l'Islam.* Paris.

Nerlich, D. 1999: *Diplomatische Gesandtschaften zwischen Ost- und Westkaisern 756–1002.* Bern.

Nicolaysen, N. 1882: *The Viking-Ship Discovered at Gokstad in Norway – Langskibet fra Gokstad ved Sandefjord.* Kristiania.

Northedge, A. & Kennet, D. 1994: The Samarra Horizon, in E.J. Grube (ed.), *Cobalt and Lustre: The First Centuries of Islamic Pottery*, 21–35. Oxford.

O

Oikonomides, N. 1986: *A Collection of Dated Byzantine Lead Seals.* Washington, D.C.

Olsen, B. 2003: Belligerent Chieftains and oppressed Hunters? Changing Conceptions of Interethnic Relationships in Northern Norway during the Iron Age and Early Medieval Period, in J.H. Barrett (ed.), *Contact, Continuity, and Collapse: The Norse Colonization of the North Atlantic*, 9–32. Turnhout.

Özsait-Kocabaş, I. 2011a: Akdeniz Gemi Yapım Geleneğinde Bir Ortaçağ Teknesi: Yenikapı 12 Batığı, in H. Şahin, E. Konyar & G. Ergin (eds), Özsait Armağanı, Mehmet ve Nesrin Özsait Onuruna Sunulan Makaleler, 345–351. Antalya.

Özsait-Kocabaş, I. 2011b: The Yenikapı 12 Shipwreck: A Local Trading Vessel from the Middle Byzantine Period. Skyllis 11: 60–63.

Özsait-Kocabaş, I. 2012: Hull Characteristics of the Yenikapı 12 Shipwreck, in N. Günsenin (ed.), Between Continents. Proceeding of the Twelfth Symposium on Boat and Ship Archaeology, Istanbul 2009, 115–120. Istanbul.

Özsait-Kocabaş, I. & Kocabaş, U. 2008: V. Technological and Constructional Features of Yenikapı Shipwrecks: A Preliminary Evaluation / V. Yenikapı Batıklarında Teknoloji ve Konstrüksiyon Özellikleri: Bir Ön Değerlendirme, in U. Kocabaş 2008: 97–185.

P

Parkin, D. & Barnes, R. (eds) 2002: Ships and the development of maritime technology in the Indian Ocean. London.

Pastorello, E. (ed.) 1938: Andreas Dandolo, Chronica per extensum descripta, in G. Carducci, V. Fiorini & P. Fedele (eds), Rerum Italicarum Scriptores, XII.1. Bologna.

Pearson, M.N. 2003: The Indian Ocean. London.

Pedersen, U. 2010: I smeltedigelen – Finsmedene i vikingtidsbyen Kaupang. PhD thesis, University of Oslo.

Pestell, T. & Ulmschneider, K. (eds) 2003: Markets in Early Medieval Europe. Trading and 'Productive' sites, 650–850. Macclesfield.

Petterson, A.-M. (ed.) 2008: Spillingsskatten – Gotland i vikingatidens världshandel. Visby.

Ploug, F. 2012: Haner og skib. Nyt eksemplar af sjælden mønttype fra 800-tallets Hedeby. Nordisk Numismatisk Unions Medlemsblad 2012: 104–105.

Pomey, P., Kahanov, Y. & Reith, E. 2012: Transition from shell to skeleton in ancient Mediterranean ship-construction: analysis, problems, and future research. The International Journal of Nautical Archaeology 41.2: 235–314.

Power, T. 2012: The Red Sea from Byzantium to the Caliphate, AD 500–1000. Cairo.

Prigent, V. 2010: La politique sicilienne de Romain Ier Lécapène, in D. Barthélemy & J.-C. Cheynet (eds), Guerre et société au Moyen Âge. Byzance-Occident (VIIIe–XIIIe siècle), 63–84. Paris.

Priyanto, W.A. 2010: Conservation Research and Treatment Programs: Case Study of Ancient Boat Site in Rembang Regency, in M. Staniforth, J. Craig, S.C. Jago-on, B. Orillaneda & L. Lacsina (eds), Proceedings on the Asia-Pacific Regional Conference on Underwater Cultural Heritage, 787–798. Manila.

Pryor, J.H. 1988: Geography, technology and war: Studies in the maritime history of the Mediterranean, 649–1571. Cambridge.

Pryor, J.H. & Jeffreys, E.M. 2006: The Age of the ΔΡΟΜΩΝ. Leiden, Boston.

Pulak, C. 2007: Yenikapı Batıkları: Fırtınanın Armağanı. ArkeoAtlas 6: 128–141.

Pulak, C., Ingram, R., Jones, M. & Matthews, S. 2013: The shipwrecks of Yenikapı and their contribution to the study of ship construction, in Z. Kızıltan (ed.), Stories from the Hidden Harbour. Shipwrecks of Yenikapı, 22–34. Istanbul.

R

Raith, M., Yule, P. & Damgaard, K. 2013: The View from Zafar: An Archaeometric Study of the Aqaba Pottery Complex and its Distribution in the 1st Millennium CE. Zeitschrift für Orient-Archäologie 6: 318–348.

Ray, H.P. & Salles, J.-F. (eds) 1996: Tradition and archaeology. Early maritime contacts in the Indian Ocean. New Delhi.

Reade, J. (ed.) 1996: The Indian Ocean in Antiquity. London.

Reiske, J.J. (ed.) 1829: Constantine VII Porphyrogenitus, De cerimoniis aulae byzantinae, I. Bonn.

Renaudot, E. (trans.) 1733: Ancient Accounts of India and China (Silsilat al-tawārīkh). London.

Rieck, F. 1998: Die Schiffsfunde aus dem Nydammoor. Alte Fund und neue Untersuchungen, in J. Bemmann & G. Bemmann (eds), Der Opferplatz von Nydam, 267–292. Neumünster.

Rispling, G. 2007: Ninth-century dirham hoards in Russia and the Baltic region: A report on progress, in M. Andersen, H.W. Horsnæs & J.C. Moesgaard (eds), Magister Monetae. Studies in Honour of Jørgen Steen Jensen, 101–109. Copenhagen.

Roesdahl, E. 1992: The Vikings. London.

Roesdahl, E. 2003: Walrus ivory and other northern luxuries: their importance for Norse voyages and settlements in Greenland and America, in S. Lewis-Simpson (ed.), Vínland Revisited: the Norse World at the Turn of the First Millennium. Selected Papers from the Viking Millennium International Symposium, 15–24 September 2000, Newfoundland and Labrador, 145–152. St. John's, NFL.

Roesdahl, E., Sindbæk, S.M., Pedersen, A. & Wilson, D. (eds) 2014: Viking Age Aggersborg: the Settlement and Fortress. Højbjerg, Copenhagen.

Rogers, J.M. 1991: Chinese Iranian Relations. ii. Islamic Period to the Mongols. Encyclopaedia Islamica 4.3, 431–434. Leiden.

Rong, X. 2011: New evidence on the history of Sino-Arabic relations: a study of Yang LIangyao's embassy to the Abbasid Caliphate. Paper presented the International Conference on Land and Maritime Communications and World Civilizations, Sun Yatsen University, December 4–5, 2011.

S

Sakelliades, V. 1997: Byzantine naval power, in D. Zafiropoulou (ed.), Journeys on the Seas of Byzantium, 47–54. Athens.

Sauvaget, J. (trans. & ed.) 1948: Akhbâr aṣ-Ṣīn wa l-Hind (Relation de la Chine et de l'Inde). Paris.

Sawyer, P. 2007: Ohthere's destinations: Norway, Denmark and England, in Bately & Englert 2007: 136–139.

Schreiner, P. 2011: Die kaiserliche Familie. Ideologie und Praxis im Rahmen der internationaler Beziehungen in Byzanz. LVIII Settimane di Studio della Fondazione Centro Italiano di Studi sull'Alto Medioevo, 735–773. Spoleto.

Scudder, B. (trans.) & Oskarsdottir, S. (ed.) 2002: Egil's Saga. London.

Sen, T. 1996: Administration of maritime trade during the Tang and Song dynasties. China Report 32: 251–265.

Shafiq, S. 2013: Seafarers of the Seven Seas: The Maritime Culture in the Kitāb Ajā'ib al-Hind by Buzurg Ibn Shahriyār (d. 399/1009). Berlin.

Sharma, R.S. 1987: Urban Decay in India (c. 300–1000). New Delhi.

Shepard, J. 1995: The Rhos guests of Louis the Pious: whence and wherefore?. Early Medieval Europe 4: 41–60.

Shepherd, G.M. 1982: The making of the Swahili: A view from the southern end of the East African coast, Paideuma 28: 129–148.

Sheriff, A. 2010: Dhow Cultures of the Indian Ocean: Cosmopolitanism, Commerce and Islam. London.

Shetelig, H. 1950: Religionshistoriske drag fra vikingetidens stilhistorie. Viking 14: 49–62.

Signes Codoñer, J. 2004: Bizancio y al-Ándalus en los siglos IX y X, in I. Pérez Martín & P. Bádenas de la Peña (eds), Bizancio y la Península Ibérica. De la Antigüedad Tardía a la Edad Moderna, 177–245. Madrid.

Sinclair, P.J.J. 1995: The origins of urbanism in East and southern Africa: A diachronic perspective, in K. Ådahl & B. Sahlström (eds), Islamic Art and Culture in Sub-Saharan Africa, 99–110. Uppsala.

Sindbæk, S.M. 2007: Networks and nodal points. The emergence of towns in Early Viking Age Scandinavia. Antiquity 81: 119–132.

Sindbæk, S.M. 2011: Silver Economies and Social Ties: Long-Distance Interaction, Long-term Investments – and why the Viking Age happened, in J. Graham-Campbell, S.M. Sindbæk & G. Williams (eds), Silver Economies, Monetisation & Society in Scandinavia, 800–1100, 41–66. Aarhus.

Sindbæk, S.M. 2014: Crossbreeding Beasts: Christian and Non-Christian Imagery in Oval Brooches, in I. Garipzanov (ed.), *Conversion and Identity in the Viking Age*, 167-193. Turnhout.

Sjøvold, T. 1974: *The Iron Age Settlement of Artic Norway*. Oslo.

Skre, D. 2007a: The Sciringeshealh of Ohthere's Time, in Bately & Englert 2007: 150-156.

Skre, D. 2007b: Towns and Markets, Kings and Central Places in South-western Scandinavia, in Skre 2007c: 445-469.

Skre, D. (ed.) 2007c: *Kaupang in Skiringssal*. Oslo, Aarhus.

Skre, D. 2008: Post-Substantivist Towns and Trade AD 600-1000, in D. Skre (ed.), *Means of Exchange. Dealing with Silver in the Viking Age*, 327-341. Aarhus.

Skre, D. 2011: Commodity Money, Silver and Coinage in Viking-Age Scandinavia, in J. Graham-Campbell, S.M. Sindbæk & G. Williams (eds), *Silver Economies, Monetisation & Society in Scandinavia, 800-1100*, 67-92. Aarhus.

Smyth, A.P. 1977: *Scandinavian Kings in the British Isles 850-880*. Oxford.

Steuer, H. 2009: Principles of trade and exchange: trade goods and merchants, in Englert & Trakadas 2009: 294-308.

Stevenson, W.H. (ed.) 1904: *Asser's Life of King Alfred*. Oxford.

Storli, I. 2007: Ohthere and his World, in Bately & Englert 2007: 76-99.

Stylegar, F.-A. 2007: The Kaupang Cemeteries Revisited, in Skre 2007c: 65-128.

T

Takakusu, J. 1896: *A Record of the Buddhist Religion as Practised in India and the Malay Archipelago (AD 671-695) by I-Tsing*. Oxford.

Al-Tanukhi, A. 1955: *Al-Faraj ba'd al-shidda*, II. Cairo, Baghdad.

Theuws, F. 2012: River-based trade centres in early medieval northwestern Europe. Some 'reactionary' thoughts, in Gelichi & Hodges 2012: 23-46.

Thomas, G. 2012: Carolingian Culture in the North Sea World: Rethinking the Cultural Dynamics of Personal Adornment in Viking-Age England. *European Journal of Archaeology* 15.3: 486-518.

Thurn, H. (ed.) 1973: *John Skylitzes, Synopsis Historion*. Berlin, New York.

Tibbetts, G.R. (trans.) 1971: *Arab navigation in the Indian Ocean before the coming of the Portuguese: being a translation of Kitāb al-fawāʾidf i uṣūl al-baḥr waʾl-qawāʿid of Aḥmad b. Mājid al-Najdī*. London.

Tsougarakis, D. 1988: *Byzantine Crete from the 5th Century to the Venetian Conquest*. Athens.

V

Van der Lith, P.A. (ed.) & Devic, L.M. (trans.) 1883-1886: *Buzurg b. Shahriyār, Kitāb ʿajaʾib al-Hind: barruhu, wa-baḥruhu wa-jazāʾiruhu (Livre des merveilles de l'Inde)*. Leiden.

Van Es, W.A. & Verwers, W.J.H. 1980: *Excavations at Dorestad 1. The Harbour: Hoogstraat I*. Amersfoort.

Varenius, B. 1992: *Det nordiska skeppet. Teknologi och samhällsstrategi i vikingatid och medeltid*. Stockholm.

Varenius, B. 1994: The Hedeby Coinage. *Current Swedish Archaeology* 2: 185-194.

Vasiliev, A.A. 1935: *Byzance et les Arabes. La dynastie d'Amorium (820-867)*, I. Brussels.

Vosmer, T. 1999. Indo-Arabian stone anchors in the western Indian Ocean and Arabian Sea. *Arabian archaeology and epigraphy* 10: 248-263.

Vosmer, T. 2010: The Jewel of Muscat: reconstructing a ninth-century sewn-plank boat, in Krahl et al. 2010: 121-135.

W

Wallace, B. 2011: L'Ance aux Meadows: different disciplines, divergent views, in S. Sigmundsson (ed.), *Viking Settlements and Viking Society. Papers from the Proceedings of the 16th Viking Congress*, 448-468. Reykjavik.

Wang, G. 2003: *The Nanhai Trade: The Early History of Chinese Trade in the South China Sea*. Singapore.

Wang, G.W. 1958: The Nanhai trade. A study of the early history of Chinese trade in the South China Sea. *Journal of the Malaysian Branch of the Royal Asiatic Society* 31: 1-135.

Wheatley, P. 1961: *The Golden Khersonese*. Kuala Lumpur.

Whitcomb, D. 1998: Out of Arabia: Early Islamic Aqaba in its regional context, in R.P. Gayraud (ed.), *Colloque International d'Archéologie Islamique*, 403-418. Cairo.

Whitcomb, D. 2009: Ayla at the Millennium: Archaeology and History, in F. al-Khraysheh (ed.), *Studies in the History and Archaeology of Jordan* 10, 123-132. Amman.

Whitehouse, D. 1970: Siraf: a medieval port on the Persian Gulf. *World Archaeology* 2.2: 141-158.

Whitehouse, D. 1980: *Siraf III. The Congregational Mosque and Other Mosques from the Ninth to the Twelfth Centuries*. London.

Whitehouse, D. 1983: Maritime trade in the Gulf: The eleventh and twelfth centuries. *World Archaeology* 14: 328-334.

Whitehouse, D. 2001: East Africa and the Maritime Trade of the Indian Ocean, A.D. 800-1500, in B. Scarcia Amoretti (ed.), *Islam in East Africa: new sources*, 411-424. Rome.

Whitehouse, D. 2009: *Siraf. History, Topography and Environment*. Oxford.

Whitehouse, D. & Williamson, A. 1973: Sasanian Maritime Trade. *Iran* 11: 29-49.

Whitelock, D. 1996 (2nd edn): *English historical documents, c. 500-1042*. London.

Whitewright, J. 2009: The Mediterranean lateen sail in late antiquity. *The International Journal of Nautical Archaeology* 38.1: 97-104.

Whitewright, J. 2011: The Potential Performance of Ancient Mediterranean Sailing Rigs. *International Journal of Nautical Archaeology* 40.1: 2-17.

Whittow, M. 1996: *The Making of Orthodox Byzantium, 600-1025*. Basingstoke.

Wickham, C. 2005: *Framing the Early Middle Ages*. Oxford.

Williams, G. 2010: The influence of Dorestad coinage on coin design in England and Scandinavia, in A. Willemsen & H. Kik (eds), *Dorestad in an international framework*, 105-111. Turnhout.

Willroth, K.-H. 1992: *Untersuchungen zur Besiedlungsgeschichte der Landschaften Angeln und Schwansen von der älteren Bronzezeit bis zum frühen Mittelalter: Eine Studie zur Chronologie und Siedlungskunde*. Neumünster.

Wink, A. 2002: *Al-Hind, the Making of the Indo-Islamic World. Vol. 1: Early Medieval India and the Expansion of Islam 7th–11th Centuries*. Leiden.

Wołoszyn, M. (ed.) 2009: *Byzantine Coins in Central Europe between the 5th and 10th Century*. Krakow.

Wolters, O.W. 1958: Tambralinga. *Bulletin of the School of Oriental and African Studies* 21: 587-607.

Wolters, O.W. 1967: *Early Indonesian Commerce: A Study of the Origins of Srivijaya*. Ithaca, London.

Wong Wai Yee 2010: *A Preliminary Study of Some Economic Activities of Khmer Empire: Examining the Relationship between the Khmer and Guangdong Ceramic Industries during 9th to 14th Centuries*. PhD thesis, National University of Singapore.

Wood, M. 2011: *Interconnections: Glass Beads and Trade in Southern and Eastern Africa and the Indian Ocean, 7th to 16th Centuries A.D.* Uppsala.

Wright, H.T. 1993: Trade and Politics on the eastern littoral of Africa, AD800-1300, in T. Shaw, P.J.J. Sinclair, B. Andah & A. Okpoko (eds), *The Archaeology of Africa: food, metals and towns*, 658-670. London.

Wyatt, D. 2009: *Slaves and warriors in medieval Britain and Ireland, 800-1200*. Leiden.

Yahya, M.B.H. 2005: *The boats of Brunei Darussalam*. Bandar Seri Begawan. Brunei.

Yule, H. (trans.) 1914: *Cathay and the Way Thither. Being a collection of medieval notices of China*. London.

Z

Zachrisson, T. 2012: The archaeology of Rimbert. The churches of Hergeir and Gautbert and Borg in Birka, in S. Sigmundsson (ed.), *Viking Settlements and Viking Society. Papers from the Proceedings of the Sixteenth Viking Congress*, 469-493. Reykjavik.

Zangemeister, C. (ed.) 1882: *Pauli Orosii, Historiarum adversum Paganos Libri Septem*. Vienna.

Index

Abbasid/Abbasids/Abbasid Caliphate 10, 44, 46–47, 49, 65, 69, 83, 98, 109–110, 114

Aylah 8, 10, 44, 46, 63, 95, 106–107

Borobudur 8, 44, 57, 115–118

Byzantine/Byzantines/Byzantine Empire 8–10, 27, 35, 47, 55, 68–81, 83–85, 87–91, 103, 109

China 8–10, 39–49, 51, 55–56, 58–59, 63, 95, 99, 107–113, 115–118, 120–124

Constantinople 8–10, 68–72, 74–76, 78–80, 83, 86–88, 90, 95, 103, 109

Denmark 8, 18, 31, 33–34, 36–37, 65, 73, 88, 101

East Africa 10, 41, 43, 49, 51–52, 55, 63–64, 109, 111, 113–114, 123–124

Emporia 11, 22–25, 34, 37, 51, 53, 73, 111, 113, 123, 125

England 8, 11, 101, 103–104

Franks/Francia/Frankish Empire/Frankish Kingdom 8, 10, 20–21, 23, 34–35, 67, 72–73, 70–76, 83, 95, 97, 104, 125

Germany 8, 20–22, 34–35, 37, 72–73, 88

Hålogaland 8, 18–19, 21, 25, 28–29, 96

Hedeby 8, 18–24, 28–29, 31, 37, 70–71, 73, 75, 88–89, 91, 98, 102–105, 125

India 8, 10–11, 39–41, 43–46, 48, 51, 55, 57, 61, 63–64, 95, 109, 112–113, 115–117, 120, 122–124

Indonesia 9, 41, 45, 55, 58, 108, 115–120, 123, 125

Iran/Persia 8, 41–43, 45–49, 53, 61, 65, 107, 109–110, 115, 117, 120–123

Ireland 8, 18–20, 27, 29, 100

Italy 69, 72, 74, 77

Java 8, 10–11, 40, 43–44, 57, 115–120, 124–125

Kaupang 8, 19–21, 23, 25, 28–29, 75, 96–97

Norway 8, 17–21, 25, 27–31, 36–37, 96–97, 100, 103, 125

Piracy/pirates 8, 10, 22, 28–29, 45, 68–69

Ports 8, 10–11, 15, 18, 20, 34–35, 42–43, 46–49, 51, 55, 63–64, 68–69, 75, 78–81, 83–84, 86–87, 106, 109–110, 116–118, 120–121

Rus/Russia 9, 69–71, 73, 89, 98

Saxons 15, 18, 103

Scandinavia/Scandinavians 8–9, 11, 15, 20–29, 31–37, 65, 69, 71, 91, 97–98, 100, 104–105, 125

Seafaring 8–11, 26, 28, 31, 43, 45, 63, 97, 118, 120

Ship/s 8–11, 17, 20, 22, 24, 26–32, 34, 41–45, 47–48, 55–57, 59, 61, 63, 69, 71–72, 75, 78–87, 96, 101–105, 109–110, 115–120, 124

Siraf 8–10, 41–49, 51, 55, 57–58, 63, 95, 108–110, 116

Sri Lanka 44, 47, 128, 123–124

Srivijaya Empire 44, 115–118, 124

Suzhou 8, 44, 121–123

Swahili/Swahili coast 44, 51–53, 114

Tang Dynasty 10, 44, 46–47, 49, 55, 110, 120–123

Tanzania 53–53, 63–64, 95, 111

Trade 8, 10–11, 18–19, 22–27, 31, 33–35, 40, 42–55, 64–65, 69–70, 73, 75–87, 96–104, 106–110, 113, 115–116, 118, 121, 124

Truso 8, 19, 23, 27, 29, 98–99

Turkey 10, 69, 81–82, 84, 86, 95

Venice 8, 68–69, 71–77, 83, 85, 87

Viking Age/Viking 7–11, 14, 20–21, 23–28, 32, 65, 73, 95, 98–100, 105

Zanzibar 8, 10, 41, 44, 46, 53, 63–64, 111–114

List of Authors

Dionisius A. Agius
University of Exeter, U.K./
King Abdulaziz University, Saudi Arabia
dion.agius@googlemail.com

Steven P. Ashby
University of York, U.K.
steve.ashby@york.ac.uk

Janet Bately
King's College London, U.K.
janet.bately@kcl.ac.uk

Mateusz Bogucki
Polish Academy of Sciences, Poland
matbogu@yahoo.com

J.-C. Cheynet
Collège de France, France
jean-claude.cheynet@college-de-france.fr

Ashley Coutu
Aarhus University, Denmark
anc@hum.au.dk

Sarah Croix
Aarhus University, Denmark
marksc@hum.au.dk

Alison Crowther
University of Oxford, U.K.
alison.crowther@rlaha.ox.ac.uk

Kristoffer Damgaard
University of Copenhagen, Denmark
kd@hum.ku.dk

Anton Englert
Viking Ship Museum in Roskilde, Denmark
ae@vikingeskibsmuseet.dk

Sauro Gelichi
University of Ca' Foscari – Venice, Italy
gelichi@unive.it

Jeremy Green
Western Australian Museum, Australia
jeremy.green@museum.wa.gov.au

Jason Hawkes
Aarhus University, Denmark
hawkes.jason@gmail.com

Helle Horsnæs
National Museum, Denmark
Helle.Horsnaes@natmus.dk

Mark Horton
University of Bristol, U.K.
Mark.Horton@bristol.ac.uk

Sven Kalmring
Center for Baltic and Scandinavian
Archaeology, Germany
kalmring@schloss-gottorf.de

Ole Thirup Kastholm
Roskilde Museum, Denmark
Olekast@roskilde.dk

Sorna Khakzad
University of Leuven, Belgium/
East Carolina University, U.S.A.
sorna_serena@yahoo.com

Jun Kimura
Field Museum of Natural
History Chicago, U.S.A.
jkimura@fieldmuseum.org

Ufuk Kocabaş
Istanbul University, Turkey
ufukkocabas@gmail.com

Chris Lowe
Headland Archaeology, U.K.
chris.lowe@headlandarchaeology.com

John N. Miksic
National University of Singapore,
Singapore
seajnm@nus.edu.sg

J.C. Moesgaard
National Museum, Denmark
jens.christian.moesgaard@natmus.dk

Işıl Özsait-Kocabaş
Istanbul University, Turkey
isilkocabas@yahoo.com.tr

Unn Pedersen
University of Oslo, Norway
unn-pedersen@iakh.uio.no

Tim Power
Zayed University, United Arab Emirates
timothy.power@zu.ac.ae

Jonathan Shepard
Cambridge University, U.K.
nshepard@easynet.co.uk

Søren M. Sindbæk
Aarhus University, Denmark
farksms@hum.au.dk

Athena Trakadas
Viking Ship Museum in Roskilde, Denmark/
University of Southern Denmark, Denmark
trakadas@sdu.dk

Dries Tys
Vrije Universiteit Brussel, Belgium
dtys@vub.ac.be

Tom Vosmer
Ministry of Heritage and Culture,
Sultanate of Oman
tom@muheet.com.au

Julian Whitewright
University of Southampton, U.K.
r.j.whitewright@soton.ac.uk

Stephanie Wynne-Jones
University of York, U.K.
stephanie.wynne-jones@york.ac.uk

Previous page: *Jewel of Muscat*, a reconstruction of the Belitung wreck, in the Indian Ocean, 2010 (Photo: Robert Jackson).